DEAR ROBERT,                                    2016

MAY BOTH YOUR PASSION FOR "LETTERS"
& CREATIVE SPIRIT BE INSPIRED BY
THIS BOOK.

MAY YOUR CURIOSITY, WORK ETHIC &
PERSEVERANCE GIVE YOU THE COURAGE
TO TAKE RISKS & WITHSTAND CHALLENGES
FROM THE STATUS QUO.

MAY YOUR VISION HELP SHAPE OUR
CULTURE, AND YOUR PURSUITS CONTINUE
TO DELIGHT BOTH YOU & OTHERS.

CONGRATULATIONS ON YOUR INDUCTION
INTO THE CENTURY CLUB, AND BEST
WISHES ON BEING OUTSTANDING IN
YOUR FIELD OF CHOICE & EXCEPTIONAL
IN MANY AREAS.

We're so proud of you!

Tom & ♡ Amy

# The Renaissance Man's Manifesto

1. I am outstanding in my field *and* exceptional in many areas.
2. I am insatiably curious.
3. I embrace culture.
4. I merge my left brain and my right brain.
5. I delight in sharing what I do.
6. I have the courage to take risks.
7. I create.
8. I persevere.
9. I am passionate.
10. I have vision.
11. I challenge the status quo.
12. I shape the future.

**I am a Renaissance Man.**

# BEYOND GENIUS©

The 12 Essential Traits

*of*

Today's Renaissance Men©

*Scott Griffiths and Eric Elfman*

AuthorHouse™
1663 Liberty Drive
Bloomington, IN 47403
www.authorhouse.com
Phone: 1-800-839-8640

Published by AuthorHouse 4/15/2013

ISBN: 978-1-4817-0294-2 (sc)
ISBN: 978-1-4817-0293-5 (hc)
ISBN: 978-1-4817-0292-8 (e)

Library of Congress Control Number: 2012924135

This book is printed on acid-free paper. Printed in the United States of America. For information, address The Griffiths Organization, 30821 Seminole Place, Laguna Niguel, CA 92677.

www.TodaysRenaissanceMen.com

Edited by Dale Griffiths Stamos
Cover Design by Debbie Yudkin
Interior Design and Research by Alexa Espinoza

Expanded First Edition

*This book is dedicated to*
Dave Carpenter

# CONTENTS

# Part Three | **Contemporary Renaissance Men**

# FOREWORD

## By Dave Stewart

For years I have jumped between all these worlds. From music, to business, to television, to charity, to well... you get the picture. People would say things to me like: How do you juggle them all? Or... You shouldn't do all these different things. You should just play guitar, or just write songs. And I was never able to understand that.

I was talking about it one day, back in 1989, to Bob Geldof (originator of *Live Aid*), and he said, "Well, that's because you're a *fecking* polymath," (supply your own Irish accent). Then he said... "I'm a *fecking* polymath too." And he is. Bob is always doing a hundred things at the same time, like me.

So when I heard the description of this book about Renaissance Men, about these people from the past and the present, and the things about them, the ways their minds work, that allow them to do so many creative things at the same time, I was intrigued.

If you look at children, you see they are all Renaissance people in the making. They go flying into everything, and they have no fear of failing. The Renaissance Men of the past and the present, they're like that. They just keep going at things, no matter what. People talk about thinking outside the box? Well, for me, I never even saw a box. I was just always dreaming. But kids are discouraged from dreaming, and certainly from thinking against the system.

This book will give you a look inside the Renaissance personality, what make them tick, and that's important. Because I think there's a crisis in our society in terms of creativity - where the very things that make a dreamer become an entrepreneur, for example, has not been written into the equation that allows a country to be one step ahead. The acceleration of technology, and the way that knowledge is consumed, the need to create new businesses to create thousands of jobs, well that may not necessarily come from a big established company, it will come from a Renaissance thinker. That's who will come up with an idea nobody else has thought of.

When I was growing up, I was never taught anything about business, or entrepreneurship, or how to come up with an invention, or an idea. At 11 years old, in Sunderland, England, I went to this prestigious grammar school. But still, they didn't incentivize you to use your imagination in any way. They didn't put a link between what you can dream and how you can act. There was a kind of system in place where you were segregated into roles at the age of 11. Section for plumbers. Section for math types, etc. But no one said: "Oh, he's a dreamer, that's a great job." They just said, if you want to learn about this, there's only one way to do it. Well, I was one of those kids who would raise my hand and ask: "Why? Why does it have to be like that?" And then I'd get to spend the next three hours standing at the blackboard with my nose on this one spot.

I think it's getting better today. Around the beginning of the Internet, we began to see and read about people who were visionaries, thinking about things in a completely different way, and becoming successful. People like Richard Branson, for example, or the kids who came up with Facebook, or Blake Mycoskie who came up with Tom's Shoes. Today, someone can sit in a bedroom and dream up an idea, and with the tools on a laptop, they can make it all happen. Back in my day, if you had a dream of something, it was very difficult to get people to understand that it could be possible. For me, being a rock star was one way I could prove myself. I said: "I'm going to travel the world and play in stadiums." And then people looked at me and said: Yeah, he actually did that. Well, now, someone can write a blog and say they're going to build wells in Africa" and the response is: "Hey, that's cool!" and they have no problem believing it's going to happen.

Still we have a long way to go to really accept the Renaissance ideal. We need more of our own da Vincis and Michelangelos. People who dream up whole new worlds. We need these unusual, out of the box thinkers who don't quite seem to fit into the system, but who are the ones who really shake things up. These are the ones who are going to create the jobs and opportunities of the future, the ones who'll really bring new possibilities! Think about whoever dreamt up the Internet. How many people are actually employed through the Internet? Hundreds of millions, right?

So, if we look at our education system now, is it doing all it can to encourage these new kinds of thinkers? Ken Robinson, the education specialist, describes how the uniqueness in certain kids is often overlooked, or worse, given pejorative labels. He described this little girl who was driving the teachers mad, and they kept saying there's something wrong with her, she can't stay still, just fidgets all the time. The parents took her to all kinds of specialists and finally they went to this one doctor and the doctor said, "Can I just talk to her alone for a minute?", and after five or ten minutes they went back in and he says, "I've worked it all out. She's a dancer." In this other story, Ken talks about another girl, very quiet, rather anxious and nervous, who, one day, was furiously drawing. So the teacher went up to her and said: "What are you drawing?" The little girl said: "A picture of God." And the teacher said: "Nobody knows what God looks like," and she said, "They will in a minute."

The point is, Ken Robinson has shown that there are lots of people out there who are potential Renaissance thinkers and it actually gets beaten out of them. Think of the film, Billy Elliott. Interestingly, I'm exactly from where he's from and from the same time. I wanted to play the guitar and write songs and he wanted to dance. But this desire of his didn't fit with what was happening around him and his dad thought he was crazy.  But he stuck it out. He couldn't help it, it was his passion. And then one day his Dad saw him dance at the ballet, in London, and it made him cry. One of the things that saved Billy is that, despite being in this tough mining community, there was this one woman, this teacher, who recognized his gift and inspired him.

That's what we need more of: teachers and mentors who can spot and encourage these remarkable kids before they get swallowed up by the system. I remember something that happened at my school that saved my bacon. There was a teacher, Dick Bradshaw, the English teacher, who secretly wanted to be a jazz pianist. So he kind of taught English like a jazz lesson - it was all over the place. But me, I could follow him. My mind worked like that. He really got through to me, and later we became friends. When I'd go to his house and he'd play songs on the piano, it made me realize that I could actually do music too. The first song I ever recorded was one of his songs.

Now of course, he wasn't the music teacher. The music teacher threw a hymn book at me, which was a brand new one, and the two spikes of the corner went into my head and I had to get stitches. So that wasn't much of a music lesson. In the end, it was the teacher who had passion who inspired me, not the so-called expert.

So I think this book about Renaissance Men, both past and present, and the traits that they all share in common, is really important. If teachers, and parents, and society in general for that matter, start to see that traits like creativity, or challenging the system, or passion, or curiosity, or right/left brain thinking are all essential to a Renaissance personality, to someone who can be our next Steve Jobs, or Elon Musk, I would think they will be a lot more prone to stop marginalizing these traits and begin to see them for what they are - absolutely crucial to our future as a society.

When I write a song, I hope that people go away, after hearing it, seeing less boundaries. That their dreams open up to them. That the horizon or landscape changes for their personal future. That is what I hope this book will do as well.

*Dave Stewart*
Weapons Of Mass Entertainment
www.weaponsofme.com

# PREFACE

This book rose out of a question. What, really, is a Renaissance Man? Most people define a Renaissance Man as an individual who excels in a number of areas. But is this, in fact, too limiting a definition? Is a Renaissance Man or the state of Renaissance-ness, something more than that? Is it also something that goes beyond IQ, or straight intelligence? We, of course, have our rocket scientists, and concert pianists, and remarkable people of enormous intellect and talent. These are our geniuses and they are to be admired and encouraged. But is the Renaissance personality something that goes beyond genius, because it is not just one skill or brilliance in one thing, but instead a multitude of interacting skills and traits that together empower Renaissance Men to be the visionaries, groundbreakers, and prodigious achievers that they are?

I began to explore some of these questions a number of years ago. As a successful marketing executive, brand strategist, and entrepreneur with a BFA from Art Center College of Design, I decided to further enhance my skills by pursuing an MBA from the Anderson School of Business at UCLA. As an artist and designer, I had studied many of the great Renaissance men and found them fascinating. Not just for their art, but for the fertility and breadth of who they were. Now, during my first year at the Anderson School, I had one of those aha! moments. This was the Executive MBA Program so most of my fellow students were in their thirties, and were top engineers from companies such as Boeing, Hughes, and Raytheon. These guys were all brilliant…some even geniuses, so smart that they spoke in algorithms. I mean, you have to be pretty smart to speak in algorithms! I had chosen the Anderson School because I knew my right brain was pretty well developed. And in terms of left brain, I had always been very good at math and science, but I wanted to be exposed more specifically to a prestigious university respected for its commitment to analytic thinking. This would be an opportunity to further develop a left brain focus. Well, beware of what you ask for, because during that first year, it was extreme left brain! The curriculum was advanced statistics, quantitative analysis, operational systems, supply chain management, and advanced levels of finance and accounting. While most of the engineers were breezing through the material, I barely got through. My self-esteem took a dive and I found myself thinking: What am I doing here?

The aha! moment came in the second year when the curriculum transitioned into marketing, strategy, digital concepts, and human resources. Well, these genius engineers that I admired so much, literally fell apart. To them, the soft stuff was the hard stuff. And that is when I realized: yes they are brilliant, but they are not brilliant at everything! Maybe being too much in one direction is not so valuable—at least not in today's multi-faceted, ever evolving world.

Then, a number of years later, as I was nationally expanding my chain of 18/8 Fine Men's Salons, I started to ask the question from a more active standpoint. I said, well I want the brand to be aspirational, I want to be able to make a statement about "Man at his Best", and realized that for me, that "best" was a Renaissance Man.

It was then that the idea for a book about Renaissance Men began to come into focus. I approached Eric Elfman. Eric is a distinguished writer who has published 12 books. With my four published books, we had 16 between us—and five best sellers. Eric and I had been working together on two other book projects (which are still in development), and we complemented each other well. I also knew this book needed to capture the stories of the Renaissance Men, the rich tapestry of their lives, in all their struggles and triumphs. In other words, to do these men justice, I needed to team up with a great storyteller, and Eric Elfman is a great storyteller.

So then the serious work began. Interestingly, the book did not start out with the twelve traits that are now at its center. Our initial intent was simply to celebrate the lives of Renaissance Men, past and present. We began by researching and identifying Renaissance Men throughout history and extracting their stories. But the more we examined their lives, the more we began to observe certain traits appearing over and over again.

Then, as we looked at the Renaissance Men of today navigating through a contemporary world with its own set of challenges and societal pressures, we were struck by the realization that the same traits kept consistently emerging.

After carefully compiling and honing a list of 18 potential traits, we sought further corroboration through interviews with experts and through national surveys. This helped us cull the list down to the 12 Essential Traits that appear in this book.

Furthermore, we hope, in the examination of these Renaissance traits, that we show the importance of cultivating them in our young talent, in business, science, humanities, and in our education system.

These are the key issues we explore in this book. This is an adventure of discovery—one that I hope will open your eyes in ways both enlightening and profound. As you read about these extraordinary men of the past and present, and how the twelve traits manifested in their lives, our wish is that you will be inspired to identify and encourage Renaissance Men in the making, as well as very possibly uncovering your own Renaissance Man within.

*W. Scott Griffiths*

# INTRODUCTION

### Defining the Renaissance Man

*"A man can do all that he will."*

This distillation of the Renaissance ideal—the concept that a man can do anything he truly sets his mind to, that he can develop himself in mind and body without limitation—was written in the 15th century by Leon Battista Alberti.

And as if to personally prove his point, Alberti was not only a mathematician, a philosopher, a poet, a scientist, an inventor, an accomplished horseman and archer, he was also a leading architect (several 15th century buildings he designed are still standing), an acclaimed artist (his 1436 book, *On Painting*, formalized the rules of perspective), and a Roman Catholic priest.

Yet Alberti did not consider himself extraordinary. He championed Renaissance humanism, the belief that every man has the capacity to achieve greatness across a wide spectrum of talents and abilities. It only requires passion, persistence and, of course, the will, to become the ideal Renaissance Man.

The concept of a Renaissance Man (if not the term) has existed existed from the dawn of civilization through the actual Renaissance to today. Before the Renaissance, such an exceptional individual was referred to as a "Universal Man" or "polymath" (from the Greek for "one who has learned much.")

As we explored the traits shared by the historical individuals we identified as Renaissance Men, we saw that it was the synergy of these traits that made each of those individuals greater than the sum of their parts. Because of the unique interplay of these elements of their personalities, these men were able to transform both the times that they lived in and the future.

These traits, we also found, often survived parental, societal, or religious pressures. These men we admire from the past didn't just sail through their lives, brilliant from the moment of birth. It was in their struggles to express and develop these key traits that they evolved and grew into the amazing figures we now know them to be.

And it was no different as we looked at our current world and realized that the Renaissance Men of the present, those that have made astounding contributions to many areas of science, art, and technology, have, like their forebears, not always been embraced for their Renaissance instincts. Yet because of who they were and are, because they embraced and manifested the essential traits, they prevailed and rose above the crowd to accomplish extraordinary things.

The discovery that these traits are constant through time and are expressed in the lives of both historic and modern Renaissance Men is, in our opinion, a remarkable one. If there are consistent attributes that define a Renaissance individual both in the past and now, then by knowing and cultivating these traits, individuals can recognize and realize their Renaissance potential, parents and teachers can nurture and promote the Renaissance Men of tomorrow, and society can re-evaluate its approach to over-specialization.

NOTE: You may wonder why we seem to be ignoring "Renaissance Women" in our examination. It is not for lack of fascination about women who have, in the past and present, developed themselves in multiple fields and have made significant contributions to the world. On the contrary, we feel this is a subject in itself, and deserves its own special study.

# The Renaissance Man's Manifesto

---

1. I am outstanding in my field *and* exceptional in many areas.
2. I am insatiably curious.
3. I embrace culture.
4. I merge my left brain and my right brain.
5. I delight in sharing what I do.
6. I have the courage to take risks.
7. I create.
8. I persevere.
9. I am passionate.
10. I have vision.
11. I challenge the status quo.
12. I shape the future.

**I am a Renaissance Man.**

# I

## The 12 Essential Traits

In "The Renaissance Man's Manifesto," we listed the twelve traits that consistently appear in the lives of the historical Renaissance Men we examined. Here we explore these traits in more detail, noting some of the unique ways in which they manifested in the past, and also recognizing them as a template for determining the Renaissance Men of today.

# 1

I am outstanding in my field and
exceptional in many areas

*"The greater danger for most of us lies not in setting our aim too high and falling
short; but in setting our aim too low and achieving our mark."*
-- Michelangelo

The first essential trait is the one we all associate with the concept
of a Renaissance Man: he is, by definition, not only an authority in
his own profession; he is accomplished in a number of areas. He is, in
short, a man of many talents.

This trait is the ante, the price of admission, the bar. One cannot
excel at just one thing and be considered a true Renaissance Man.

Unlike the Jack-of-all-trades who is master of none, the
Renaissance Man puts the time in to gain mastery of all his interests,
and the range can be wide. Galileo invented the protocols of modern
science, wrote several earth-shaking books, *and* was a professor of fine

art; Benjamin Franklin was one of the Founding Fathers of the United States *and* invented bifocal glasses. Isaac Newton was a physicist, theologian, *and* member of Parliament.

Renaissance Men know that specialization is not a requirement of success. They ignore the naysayers and the pigeon-holers and pursue all their passions, no matter how many. They challenge the concept that talent must be limited or limiting, and embrace instead the full expression of themselves.

# 2

---

## I am insatiably curious

*"The capacity to be puzzled is the premise of all creation,*
*be it in art or in science."*
-- Erich Fromm

When Benjamin Franklin was a young man, he began the nation's first lending library—mainly so he could get his hands on more books, precious items and rare in those days. Thomas Jefferson (the "living embodiment of an inquisitive mind"[1]) owned so many books that his personal library became the core of the Library of Congress when he sold it to the U.S. government.

---

[1] Stanley Fish, "Does Curiosity Kill More Than the Cat," The New York Times, Sept. 14, 2009, quoting James A. Leach, Chairman of the National Endowment for the Humanities http://opinionator.blogs.nytimes.com/2009/09/14/does-curiosity-kill-more-than-the-cat/

Curiosity is an indispensable trait of the Renaissance Man. Through reading, personal experience and education, he seeks to know all he can about this world.

At the same time, for the Renaissance Man, an advanced education is overrated. As Albert Einstein put it, "It is a miracle that curiosity survives formal education." Both Leonardo da Vinci and Benjamin Franklin received only basic educations in their youths, and it was only when they grew older that they got their hands on books and taught themselves history, literature, math, and more. With their curiosity driving them to attain knowledge, they each become a self-taught man (or *autodidact*).

While many people are naturally curious, that doesn't make them all Renaissance Men. The key is a "dynamic curiosity"—a curiosity that leads to an active pursuit of knowledge, a search for answers that leads to more questions, which leads to the pursuit of more knowledge, and so on—in other words: a hunger for learning. We may all be born with unlimited curiosity, but at some age, through family pressures or societal forces, the urge to explore our world is dampened and depleted in most of us. But not in the Renaissance Man.

# 3

## I embrace culture

*"A nation's culture resides in the hearts and in the soul of its people."*
-- Mahatma Gandhi

The Renaissance Man does not live in an ivory tower, in a world of thought far removed from the everyday concerns of his society. Even Galileo had to work for a living, and he spent time in *actual* towers (including a particular leaning tower).

The Renaissance Man is immersed in his culture. Like Imhotep, he is engaged in his society's development, its goals and aspirations. Like Isaac Newton, he is well read, up-to-date, and interested in other people and places. He pays close attention to the politics of the day. He traces societal forces, sees trends in the arts, sciences, and commerce. He understands and appreciates both high culture and low. And he is more likely than not to see the opportunity in everything he sees and hears.

The Renaissance Man also understands culture to mean refinement and good taste. While he can make do with a loaf of bread or a bowl of rice, he enjoys the fruits of culture: he knows the pleasures of a fine meal of osso bucco over wild rice and a glass of perfectly aged Bordeaux.

And he is discerning—the Renaissance Man rarely engages in small talk just to pass the time. If he takes part in a conversation, he embraces it with his full attention. When he reads, he does not enjoy fluff as much as an in-depth article on a scientific or cultural discovery. The Renaissance Man is constantly pushing himself to experience more of his world.

While the Renaissance Man embodies his own culture, he knows it does not contain the sum of humanity's art and knowledge, or have all the answers. So he travels. He explores. Like Benjamin Franklin and Thomas Jefferson did in their day, who sought to understand cultures other than their own. It is not unusual for the Renaissance Man to speak and read several languages. He not only values other cultures, but learns from them all he can.

# 4

---

## I merge my left brain and my right brain

*"When the brain is whole, the unified consciousness of the left and right hemispheres adds up to more than the individual properties of the separate hemispheres."*

--Roger Wolcott Sperry[1]

Many people live their lives expressing themselves principally from one side of the brain or the other. The left brain is the domain of logic, numbers, of sequential thinking, of language, of organization and linearity. The right brain is the domain of creativity, artistic inspiration, intuition, visual art, and non-linear thinking. Artists are generally considered more right brain; scientists, businessmen, and

---

[1]  Heidi Aspaturian, "New Mindset on Consciousness," *Campus*, California Institute of Technology, October 1987, interview with Sperry, the neuroscientist whose work led to the Left/Right brain hypothesis.

mathematicians more left brain. Being able to merge aspects of both right and left brain thinking greatly enhances the expression of both. And Renaissance Men consistently show this desire to operate from both hemispheres.

Leonardo da Vinci was an artist whose notebooks contained designs for scientific and technological innovations. Galileo was a scientist who used his knowledge of fine art to understand what he was seeing through his telescope.

Even when the Renaissance Man is not himself an artist or a scientist, he still immerses himself in these fields. Not everyone can be a da Vinci or a Galileo, but every Renaissance Man has found a way to support the arts and sciences. Chamundaraya, for instance, was a warrior and politician, but he commissioned a sixty-foot tall sculpture of his religion's founder which became an important cultural artifact and religious site. Richard Branson, founder of Virgin Records and Virgin Atlantic Airways, founded Virgin Galactic to encourage the development of space tourism.

In the sciences, the Renaissance Man stays current, following the newest theories and advances, sharing the excitement of the latest discoveries—whether it's a new species at the bottom of the sea, or the development of a promising new cancer treatment. Advances in science are as thrilling to him as if he, himself, supported the research—which he may well have done.

Similarly he understands that art builds connections between people, between communities, and between cultures. Art helps us to express what it means to be a human being. To the Renaissance Man, art isn't a luxury but a necessity. Art inspires us and moves us forward, and a society's commitment to the arts is one of the most important ways to gauge that society's level of enlightenment.

# 5

## I delight in sharing what I do

*"Whenever I found out anything remarkable, I have thought it my duty to put down my discovery on paper, so that all ingenious people might be informed thereof."*
-- Antonie van Leeuwenhoek

Not only does he seek out knowledge, information and experience, the Renaissance Man is happy to share what he's discovered or done. He is both interested *and* interesting.

In conversation, his knowledge is deep and layered; a spellbinding storyteller, his insights are often profound. He lights up and engages while discussing his work, his perspectives and his plans. This is one thing that separates the Renaissance Man from the Know-It-All: the Renaissance Man is not a bore.

Another thing a Renaissance Man will do that the bore will never do: he will listen to you. Whether he is sharing with his friends or his team, he loves to debate ideas, to challenge and be challenged. He knows a good discussion, like a tennis game, requires the conversation to volley back and forth.

Sharing may also take the form of becoming a mentor or teacher (or in the case of Jefferson, founding a University) whose students will carry his ideas further. Or sharing may be expressed in a more altruistic sense. Benjamin Franklin selflessly refused to take out patents for any of his inventions, because he wanted to share his innovations with humanity rather than focus on extracting profits for himself.

The Renaissance Man may share his most important discoveries or revolutionary ideas in books. Galileo was one of the world's first scientists, but it was as an author that his name and his discoveries spread throughout the world. Teddy Roosevelt shared his insights and adventures in over three dozen books. As an author, the Renaissance Man can share significant concepts, including his vision of the future, with others.

# 6

---

## I have the courage to take risks

*"Only those who risk going too far*
*can possibly find out how far they can go."*
— T.S. Eliot

This quality does not imply a willingness to simply gamble with the chips falling where they may. The Renaissance Man never takes a risk for risk's sake. When proper due diligence has been carried out and a careful risk assessment made, when the potential benefits outweigh the expected cost—only then is the Renaissance Man willing to roll the dice.

Implied in the courage to take risks is the courage to fail. In most worst case scenarios, failure leads the Renaissance Man to lessons and introspection, until he can internalize the lessons and become even more powerful.

Sometimes the Renaissance Man faces substantially higher risks, and it really is life or death.

When Galileo wrote his book describing the theory of heliocentrism, he did all he could to minimize the risk, including obtaining the prior permission of the church. Still, he knew publishing the work was fraught with risk.

Thomas Jefferson and Benjamin Franklin, along with all the signatories to the Declaration of Independence, were well aware of the risk they were taking. They calculated their chances as good, and therefore hung together. But if the colonists had lost the Revolutionary War, they would have all "hung separately."

Humanity cannot progress without these risk takers willing to take chances, pushing us further.

# 7

---

## I create

*"Imagination is the beginning of creation."*
-- George Bernard Shaw

The creative force is one of the primal urges of human beings, and being able to produce something novel is at the heart of what makes life worth living for the Renaissance Man.

Often an author, musician, artist or inventor, the Renaissance Man expresses creativity in a variety of media. Leonardo de Vinci's *Mona Lisa* is, perhaps, the most famous painting in human history; Imhotep was architect to the Pharaohs; Benjamin Franklin's inventions helped as many people as his writings liberated.

But creativity is not solely about works of art and inventions. Sometimes it is the ability to see a new approach to cracking a scientific puzzle. A new business or business model can be a creation, along with a new product or a scientific innovation, or connecting the dots in new and exciting ways. A new society is also a creation, and Thomas Jefferson's crafting of a Declaration of Independence inspired a nation to be free. Creators are artists and engineers, designers and teachers, musicians and businessmen.

# 8

---

## I persevere

*"Nothing in the world can take the place of Persistence. Talent will not; nothing is more common than unsuccessful men with talent. Genius will not; unrewarded genius is almost a proverb. Education will not; the world is full of educated derelicts. Persistence and determination alone are omnipotent."*
-- Calvin Coolidge

The unsung hero of traits, a potential Renaissance Man who has every other attribute but lacks perseverance is one you will never hear of, because he gave up too soon.

The Renaissance Man keeps moving forward, even when giving up hope may seem the better option. No matter the odds stacked against him, he is always willing to give it another try.

Perseverance, however, does not mean stubborn. Course corrections are necessary even for Renaissance Men, and goals must constantly be reevaluated. He does not give up, but he does calibrate. If one definition of insanity is doing the same thing over and over again and expecting a different result, the Renaissance Man knows that while he's exploring the same thing from every conceivable angle, the world may change and meet his solution at the nexus point.

Galileo, for instance, knew he would do no one any good, least of all himself, to be burnt at the stake. The world was not, perhaps, ready for his radical ideas in the 1600s, and so he recanted. After all, he had more to write before he died—including the book considered his masterpiece, *Two New Sciences,* which he wrote while under house arrest.

# 9

---

## I am passionate

*"Enthusiasm is one of the most powerful engines of success. When you do a thing, do it with all your might. Put your whole soul into it. Stamp it with your own personality. Be active, be energetic and faithful, and you will accomplish your object. Nothing great was ever achieved without enthusiasm."*
-- Ralph Waldo Emerson

One of the most important attributes of the Renaissance Man is his passion: both the passion to make his vision a reality, and passion in enlisting others to support his ideas.

First, it takes passion to see an idea through to fruition, whether the idea is a new stove or a new nation. Passion drives the Renaissance Man forward in the face of risks, in spite of fear, no matter the obstacles, because of a faith in the concept and a certainty in the goal. Passion is the power to make things real. The connection between the existence and non-existence of something. Passion can be the emotional component that drives the Renaissance Man, even when all looks lost.

Then, when the Renaissance Man is ready to communicate his ideas to others, to convince them to invest in or work with him, he passes this passion on to them, in the process inspiring them. Michelangelo's passion inspired a Pope to give him a ceiling on which to paint his vision, while Imhotep convinced a Pharaoh to let him build the first pyramid.

The Renaissance Man wants to feel connected to a goal larger than himself, one he truly believes in.

# 10

---

**I have vision**

*"Some men see things as they are and say 'Why?' I dream things that never were and say 'Why not?'"*
-- Robert F. Kennedy

Benjamin Franklin saw a free people. Galileo saw a world built on science and mathematics. Thomas Jefferson saw the Louisiana Purchase as a way to expand the young United States across the continent at a time no one else was thinking along those lines.

The Renaissance Man has the prescience to see where his world will be in five, or ten, or twenty or more years. Having a vision and being able to articulate it to others and persuade them to invest their time and money and energy to support that vision—these are among the hallmarks of the Renaissance Man.

To be a visionary is often to be ahead of one's time. Galileo knew that eventually science would triumph and the heliocentric view would be embraced. Blaise Pascal's calculating machine may have been too expensive to make, but he had the prescience to understand its importance to the future.

Most people see the future with little fidelity. They start to get fuzzy two weeks out. But the Renaissance Man can look years into the future and see it distinctly. There are obstacles, there are details, there are challenges, of course, but the vista is clear.

# 11

---

## I challenge the status quo

*"Here's to the crazy ones. The misfits. The rebels. The troublemakers. The round pegs in the square holes. The ones who see things differently. They're not fond of rules. And they have no respect for the status quo."*
-- Apple Computer ad

New ideas, innovations, seeing the future, doing things differently—all suggest questioning authority, a social hierarchy heavily invested in the way things are now. Imhotep challenged both the way tombs had been constructed and the way medicine had been conducted for thousands of years. Galileo's idea of an earth that was not the center of the universe threatened the authority of the church.

The status quo is usually suspicious of the multi-talented Renaissance Man, because he is willing to shake up the present in order to reach for the future. In other words, the Renaissance Man often thumbs his nose at the world's opinion.

Society itself tends to push back against those who wage the battle against ignorance. Sayings to this effect, such as "Curiosity killed the cat," reinforce the message, and the myth of Pandora's box and Mary Shelley's *Frankenstein* are overt warnings not to tamper with the workings of the unknown. The Renaissance Man refuses to bow to these societal norms. Often his answers shake up the established order, which is why he is frequently looked upon as a "troublemaker."

The Renaissance Man knows that no lasting achievement is possible by doing things the same way they have been done before.

The ability to make a difference in the world demands a challenge of the highest order to the powers-that-be.

# 12

---

## I shape the future

*"Let him who would enjoy a good future*
*waste none of his present."*
-- Roger Babson[1]

To change the direction of humanity for the better is one of the great purposes of the Renaissance Men. Whether that means independence for thirteen colonies, or teaching people how to grow their own food, the Renaissance Man has within him the vital need to push humanity forward, empowering people to take control of their lives and creating more productive relationships.

The Italian Renaissance itself changed the world. The flowering of art and culture, the new interest in learning and politics instigated the change from the rule of kings to democratic forms and to other social

---

[1]  Roger Babson was an entrepreneur and founder of Babson College in Massachusetts

forces that are commonplace to us today. It began with the Renaissance humanist ideal.

All of the Renaissance Man's essential traits are, ultimately, in the service of this one. His exceptionality in many areas leads to a wide spectrum of contributions he can make to the world. His insatiable curiosity and vision of the future lets him see how life could be improved. His passionate need to create and share his work, as well as his courage to take risks and his perseverance, are nearly always performed in pursuit of a more perfect world.

And in seeing possibilities and solutions that most do not, in diverging from and challenging the norm, the Renaissance Man is able to push society and knowledge into the future.

# II

## Historical Renaissance Men

The term "Renaissance man" first appeared in print in in W. H. Woodward's 1906 book, *Studies in Education During the Age of the Renaissance*. On page 128, Woodward describes French soldiers in Italy as profoundly impressed by Rodrigo Borgia, the epitome of "the Renaissance man."[1]

While Woodward was referring to a person of the actual Renaissance, he was also suggesting a far grander concept: the ideal, multidisciplinary man whose existence predates the term and the era. For there were "Renaissance Men" long before the Renaissance.

Exceptional men. Universal men. Polymaths.

At some point, each of these men took a look around and asked himself, "Why am I here?" How he answered that question directed the course of his life.

It's important to recall that, in spite of their extraordinary achievements, these historic Renaissance Men were human beings like ourselves, not mythic demigods or superheroes. They didn't know the future, or where their choices would lead. Like us, they had to make a living. They often took huge risks to develop into the men they became.

In the following pages, we examine these historic Renaissance Men as they expressed the scope of their talents, embraced their limitlessness, and of course, exhibited the Twelve Traits. We have notated for the reader salient examples of each of the traits, though you will no doubt notice many other expressions of the traits in their lives.

---

[1] Borgia later became Pope Alexander VI, widely reputed, it must be noted, to be the most corrupt Pope of all time.

# Imhotep

## (c. 2600 BCE)

*The first doctor and the first architect in recorded history; Vizier of the King of Egypt, administrator of the Great Palace, High Priest of Heliopolis, chief sculptor; acclaimed poet, philosopher, astronomer and sage[2].* (TRAIT #1)

If the name *Imhotep* evokes an evil force, an all-powerful immortal being with a thirst for power, you've probably seen one or more movies in Universal's *Mummy* franchise (whether its 1932 or 1999 incarnation).

But it's a bum rap. Universal used Imhotep's name to create a linen-wrapped monster, but his name actually means "The one who comes with peace, is with peace." And even though he lived three thousand years before the period that provided its name, Imhotep,

[2] Asante and Mazama, ed., Encyclopedia of African Religions, v. 1, 2008, p.337

TRAIT #1 - I am outstanding in my field and exceptional in many areas

a man of vision, creativity and passion, is the world's first known Renaissance Man.

His greatest accomplishments may have been designing and overseeing the construction of Egypt's first pyramid, the Step Pyramid at Sakaara, in 2630-2611 BC. (TRAIT #7) Before Imhotep, the kings of Egypt had been buried in simple, mud-brick tombs. But for his king, Zoser (sometimes spelled Djoser), a king of Egypt's third dynasty, Imhotep designed an innovative memorial, one that departed in dramatic ways from previous architecture, as well as being the first large stone structure ever built. (TRAIT #11) Some archeologists believe Imhotep was the first architect to use load-bearing columns as a structural element. (TRAIT #6) The Step Pyramid was so solidly built, it still exists today, over 4,600 years later. And its design was so revolutionary that it inspired the later pyramids of the 4th, 5th, and 6th Dynasties, including the great pyramids at Giza.

But as historian Toby Wilkerson notes, the building of the pyramid was just one part of a twin achievement: pyramid construction was an administrative undertaking beyond anything Egypt had previously attempted[3]. Imhotep, as Vizier to Zoser, not only conceived the project, he organized and oversaw the manpower and internal infrastructure to support it. (TRAIT #4)

Imhotep was a commoner who studied hard and learned everything he could from his society, (TRAIT #2) until he rose through the

---

[3] Toby Wilkinson, *The Rise and Fall of Ancient Egypt*, Random House, 2010

TRAIT #2 - I am insatiably curious; TRAIT #4 - I merge my left brain and my right brain; TRAIT #6 - I have the courage to take risks; TRAIT #7 - I create; TRAIT #11 - I challenge the status quo

ranks and reached the position of Vizier to the king. (TRAIT #8 & TRAIT #9) In that role, he also served as high priest of the sun god Ra. (TRAIT #3)

Additionally he was revered as a poet and philosopher, many of his sayings surviving the ages. Some attribute to him the admonition: "Eat, drink and be merry for tomorrow we shall die."

Imhotep also achieved fame as a doctor in his time. Some speculate he was also the author of the earliest medical treatise ever written, (TRAIT #5) a fairly scientific description of ailments and cures, remarkably devoid of supernatural explanations and spells. (TRAIT #10) (The earliest known copy, the so-called "Edwin Smith papyrus," was hand-lettered by a scribe in c. 1500 BCE.)

Almost incredibly, Imhotep was both the first architect and the first physician ever referred to by name in written history. He left an enormous legacy for future generations. (TRAIT #12)

James Henry Breasted, who translated the Edwin Smith Papyrus in 1930, perhaps phrased it best: "In priestly wisdom, in magic, in the formulation of wise proverbs; in medicine and architecture; this remarkable figure of Zoser's reign left so notable a reputation that his name was never forgotten."[4]

---

[4] Jimmy Dunn, "About Egyptian Pyramids,"
http://www.touregypt.net/featurestories/imhotep.htm

TRAIT #3 - I embrace culture; TRAIT #5 - I delight in sharing what I do; TRAIT #8 - I persevere; TRAIT #9 - I am passionate; TRAIT #10 - I have vision; TRAIT # 12 - I shape the future

# Chamundaraya

## (940 - 989 CE)

*Military commander of the Ganga Kingdom, noted poet and author (in two languages), scholar, Minister to the court.* (TRAIT #1)

According to folklore, Chamundaraya, the great military leader of the Ganga Kingdom in India, accompanied his mother on a pilgrimage with her guru to the capital city of Paudanapura. On the way, they stopped to camp by a small hill. That night, a goddess appeared to Chamundaraya and told him not to go to the capital. The goddess told him to aim his arrow at the tall hill nearby, and the rock it struck should be carved into a great statue.

The next morning, Chamundaraya awoke. Was it only a dream? It turned out his mother and her guru had had the exact same dream.

---

TRAIT #1 - I am outstanding in my field and exceptional in many areas

The General took his bow, aimed at the opposite hill, and let one arrow fly, striking a rock near the top.[5]

It was there that Chamundaraya conceived and financed the construction of the cultural and religious landmark for which he is most known: the massive sculpture of Gomateshwara, who was also known as Lord Bahubali, founder of the Jain religion. (TRAIT #10) (Jainism is an ancient Indian religion that advocates non-violence towards all living beings. Practitioners believe that non-violence and self-control are the means by which they can free themselves from the cycle of reincarnation.)

The artistic wonder, nearly 60 feet tall, more than one thousand years old, still exists today. It is the site of a very important Jain pilgrimage once every twelve years. The statue, one of the largest free-standing statues in the world, is carved from a single block of fine-grained white marble. Chamundaraya is widely considered responsible for one of the "Seven Wonders of India." (TRAIT #12)

Little is known of his birth, beyond his caste: he was born a Brahmin. But instead of becoming a priest, he chose to become a warrior. One of his triumphs occurred when the rebellious Prince Rajaditya in the western region waged an uprising. After several successful forays, the crafty Prince took refuge in the impregnable Fortress of Ucchangi. Undeterred, the courageous Chamundaraya led his forces against this would-be usurper, (TRAIT #6) and waged a siege against the fortress where the Prince imagined he was safe. (TRAIT #8) Chamundaraya's victory there was the stuff of legends and songs, and his fame spread throughout the then-known world. (And this was before the internet and Twitter.)

---

[5] "Jaina folksongs and legends in Karnataka", http://prasadjain.hubpages.com

TRAIT #6 - I have the courage to take risks; TRAIT #8 - I persevere;
TRAIT #10 - I have vision; TRAIT # 12 - I shape the future

Chamundaraya excelled in other fields as well. Although a military man, he wrote a book detailing the tenets of the Jain religion and the lives of 63 important early Jains. It was a popular success, partly because he wisely wrote the book in the common language, Kannada, in straightforward prose that ordinary people would understand. (TRAIT #11) The book, *Chaunda Raya Purana,* is the oldest prose work written in Kannada that still exists. (TRAIT #7) He also wrote a scholarly treatise—this time, in Sanskrit—discussing the philosophy of asceticism. (TRAIT #2) And ever ready to share, and help others, Chamundaraya supported and encouraged writers whom he believed were talented and expressed a desire to learn. One young writer he assisted, Ranna, later became an important Indian poet. (TRAIT #5)

Meanwhile, in the political arena, Chamundaraya rose to Chief Minister to the court of Ganga. (TRAIT #3) Serving three monarchs in a row, he had a direct impact on the administrative policies and direction of the kingdom. (TRAIT #4)

This early Renaissance Man embraced art, philosophy and politics, following through on every project he began (TRAIT #9) inspiring and guiding others, and leaving behind a wondrous religious icon that has inspired followers of the Jain religion ever since.

---

TRAIT #2 - I am insatiably curious; TRAIT #3 - I embrace culture;
TRAIT #4 - I merge my left brain and my right brain; TRAIT #5 - I delight in sharing what I do;
TRAIT #7 - I create; TRAIT #9 - I am passionate; TRAIT #11 - I challenge the status quo

# Leonardo da Vinci

## (1452 - 1519)

*Painter (Mona Lisa and The Last Supper, among other works); sculptor, architect, draftsman, inventor, engineer, mathematician, musician, map maker, zoologist, geologist, and philosopher.* (TRAIT #1)

The artist hired to execute the artwork rubbed his hand across the lightly textured surface of the refectory wall. He estimated the space at twenty-nine feet long and about fifteen feet high. As he considered what image to put there, the delegation of fathers from the monastery of Santa Maria delle Grazie in Milan watched him anxiously. The Fathers had agreed to commission a mural featuring some suitably religious subject, and since this wall was situated in the dining area, they preferred one that involved a meal. The artist, Leonardo da Vinci, focused on the task at hand: the blank wall in front of him. He

---

TRAIT #1 - I am outstanding in my field and exceptional in many areas

dismissed the conventional method for painting murals, fresco, because that technique involved quickly splashing large areas of fresh paint on wet plaster. He was after a subtler effect, one that could only be achieved by *sfumato*, the shading and intermingling of colors which was a technique he had perfected. He rarely did anything conventionally. (TRAIT #11) Little did he know, however, that the painting he was about to embark on, *The Last Supper*, would deliver to the art world both one of its greatest treasures and one of its greatest blows.

Leonardo da Vinci is today considered the quintessential Renaissance Man. One of the world's greatest painters, architects and inventors, he also excelled in countless other areas, including, but not limited to, music, engineering and anatomy.

But Leonardo did not start with any advantages. Born illegitimate, his parents never married (not an atypical situation in those days). His mother, Caterina, a local woman (some sources suggest she was a bar maid), went on to marry an artisan, while Leonardo's father, Ser Piero da Vinci, an official of the city of Florence, stepped up and had young Leonardo raised (from the age of five) on his family's estate.

His father provided young Leo with the basic education of that period, the same "3 R's" of time immemorial: reading, writing and arithmetic. But Leo wasn't taught the one "L"—Latin—necessary at the time for an advanced education. Still that didn't stop him. He had an unquenchable thirst for learning. (TRAIT #2) He wouldn't let others make his decisions or let circumstances get in his way: when he got older, he taught himself Latin, then advanced mathematics and philosophy. (TRAIT #8) Some scholars today believe his early deprivation led to his desire for unlimited knowledge and motivated all he did. (TRAIT #9)

---

TRAIT #2 - I am insatiably curious; TRAIT #8 - I persevere;
TRAIT #9 - I am passionate; TRAIT #11 - I challenge the status quo

At the age of 14 or 15, Leo was apprenticed to Verrocchio, the finest craftsman in Florence at the time. There Leo learned and refined his own approach to painting. It didn't take long before young Leo's painted angels were so clearly superior to his master's work, that Verrocchio quit painting.[6] Leonardo opened his own studio in 1478. (TRAIT # 7)

In 1482, da Vinci sent his resume to Ludovico Sforza, the Duke of Milan, who was seeking a military consultant. After breezily dismissing his competition, da Vinci explained why he was the best man for the job. Among his claims:

- He developed a portable ladder suitable for chasing and, when necessary, running from the enemy;
- He had devised a method for destroying the walls of every kind of fortress, even ones made of rock;
- He could provide a wide variety of mortars and smoke bombs;
- He could design and supervise construction of ships that couldn't be sunk in war by the largest guns;
- His skills in architecture were unmatched, and he could design aqueducts to transport water.
- He could sculpt in marble, bronze or clay, and paint better than anyone in the business.

Da Vinci went to work for the Duke. Although no unsinkable ships were ever forthcoming, the Duke kept him busy painting, sculpting and designing court festivals, (TRAIT #3) along with also designing buildings, weapons and machines. Leonardo's notebooks

---

[6] Vasari, *Lives of the Most Emminent Painters*

---

TRAIT #3- I embrace culture; TRAIT #7- I create

from that period are rightly famous for their sketches and drawings of inventions and marvels from his imagination that were far ahead of their time, (TRAIT #10) including: a helicopter, an alarm clock, a crane for moving large rocks from a quarry, a military tank, and more.

And of course he *could* paint better than anyone.

Leonardo would continue to make entries to his notebooks throughout his life. He filled them not only with inventions, but scientific explorations - including discoveries in anatomy, optics and hydrodynamics; as well as studies in art theory, sculpture and architecture. (TRAIT #4) For his anatomical studies, da Vinci had been given access to cadavers at the Hospital of Santa Maria Nuova. He carefully and painstakingly dissected each decaying body, detailing in meticulous drawings every layer of structure, thus overthrowing centuries of mistaken beliefs about human anatomy. When the Pope declared this practice inhumane, he switched to animals.

As a musician (he played the lyre, along with other stringed instruments), he also explored and sketched out ways to improve some of the musical instruments of his day. In fact, he considered music the second most important art in his life. He said, in his notebooks, "Music may be called the sister of painting, for she is dependent upon hearing, the sense which comes second."

Interestingly, many of his notes, by the manner in which they were laid out on the page, seem intended for publication. (TRAIT #5) Why they were not published in da Vinci's lifetime is a mystery.

---

TRAIT #4- I merge my left brain and my right brain; TRAIT #5 - I delight in sharing what I do; TRAIT #10 - I have vision

Now, in 1495, as he was about to begin his work on *The Last Supper*, Leonardo was to deliver to history one of his most powerful paintings, but one that was also flawed in its execution. It was due, in true Renaissance Man fashion, to his willingness to experiment, in his quest for a better way to do things. (TRAIT #6) Instead of fresco, he chose to work in his favored medium, oil paint, which in this case he decided to apply directly to the wall. Leonardo worked on the painting from 1495 to 1497. When complete, *The Last Supper* was declared a masterpiece. But the paint failed to adhere to the dry plaster. Mold and flaking took their toll, and within decades, the painting was a ruin. Over the centuries, many attempts have been made at restoration. But in spite of the destruction and later botched attempts at restoration, nothing has diminished the painting's fame, and the powerful effect it has had on art lovers everywhere. (TRAIT #12)

Leonardo had many extraordinary works of art still to come. One of which, of course, was the iconic *Mona Lisa*, also known as *La Gioconda*, which he began painting in 1503. This painting, thought to be the portrait of Lisa Gherardini, is remarkable for its composition, its atmosphere and of course, the enigmatic and famous "Mona Lisa smile." In this painting, da Vinci was also able to employ his technique of *sfumato* to full effect.

The expanse of da Vinci's talents in the arts and sciences was remarkable, leaving a Renaissance legacy for generations to come.

---

TRAIT #6 - I have the courage to take risks; TRAIT #12 - I shape the future.

# Michelangelo

## (1475 - 1564)

*Sculptor, painter, poet, architect, engineer; works include the statues The Pietà and David, frescos on the ceiling and altar wall of the Sistene Chapel, the design of the Laurentian Library and St. Peter's Basilica; over three hundred poems, thousands of drawings and preparatory sketches.* (TRAIT #1)

The year was 1504. Michelangelo stood in front of a mammoth statue carved from a nineteen foot tall block of marble. It was his masterpiece, *David*. In 1499, the Consuls of the Guild of Wool in Florence had commissioned Michelangelo to complete the project, begun forty years earlier as a symbol of Florentine freedom, but none were prepared for the sheer physical beauty of this statue.

Anatomically perfect, one could see each vein in David's arm, every muscle in his legs. David's beautiful, serene face stared off into the

---

TRAIT #1 - I am outstanding in my field and exceptional in many areas

distance, as if contemplating his triumph over Goliath. Michelangelo would later write, "In every block of marble I see a statue as plain as though it stood before me, shaped and perfect in attitude and action. I have only to hew away the rough walls that imprison the lovely apparition to reveal it to the other eyes as mine see it."

Now David stood in its place of honor in front of the Palazzo Vecchio. Archways had been torn down and narrow streets widened to get it there; it took forty men five days to move it through Florence. The work cemented Michelangelo's reputation as one of the greatest artists of the Renaissance.

Michelangelo was born in the small town of Caprese near Tuscany. When he was six, his mother died, and the lad was sent to live with a stonecutter and his family near a marble quarry his father owned. Michelangelo fell in love with the marble, along with the tools used to hew the slabs - glimmers of a passion for sculpture that was just emerging. (TRAIT #9)

When he returned home, he informed his father that he wished to be an artist. (TRAIT #7) His father flew into a rage. "Artists are laborers, no better than shoemakers!"[7] was the less-than-supportive response the artist later recorded in his journal.

He sent his son to study in Florence, hoping schooling would knock some sense into him. But Florence, during the Renaissance, was a vibrant center of the arts, and the young Michelangelo had no interest in going to school. Instead of attending class, he spent his

---

[7] William E. Wallace, Michelangelo: *The Artist, the Man and His Times*, 2009, Washington University

---

TRAIT #7 - I create; TRAIT #9 - I am passionate

time with artists and copied paintings in churches, voraciously learning everything he could from them. (TRAIT #2)

At the age of thirteen, he took the initiative to apprentice himself to the painter Domenico Ghirlandaio. Finally his father knew it was time to give up the fight and actually contacted Ghirlandaio, convincing the established painter to pay his son wages as an artist, a very unusual arrangement for the time.

When Lorenzo de' Medici (known as "the Magnificent") asked Ghirlandaio to send him his two best pupils, one of them was Michelangelo. For three years, he attended the arts academy founded by Medici. He studied sculpture and was exposed to the most prominent philosophers and writers of that time. This immersion into the intellectual and artistic culture of his day was heaven to the young man. (TRAIT #3)

It was at this time he made the verbal slip that caused his most prominent physical feature apparent in his later self-portraits: one day, while he and another young sculptor, Pietro Torrigiano were copying frescos in a church, Michelangelo made a disparaging crack about the quality of the other artist's work. The furious Torrigiano punched Michelangelo in the face and broke his nose.

Michelangelo carved two relief sculptures before he was sixteen, *The Madonna of the Stairs* and *The Battle of the Centaurs*. *The Madonna of the Stairs* was a tender portrait of the Virgin Mary nursing the baby Jesus. *The Battle of the Centaurs,* suggested by the mythic struggle between ancient Greeks and the Centaurs, depicts a violent chaotic clash of men. The duality of these two works is striking, as the first

---

TRAIT #2 - I am insatiably curious; TRAIT #3 - I embrace culture

reflects his deep religious faith, while the other is a pagan celebration of the male nude. This pull between the sacred and the profane would follow him his whole life.

When Medici died in 1492, Michelangelo returned home. He persuaded the prior of a church in Florence to allow him to dissect corpses awaiting burial, to better understand anatomical structures. This was a dangerous activity, now strictly forbidden by the church. But Michelangelo was willing to take the risk for the sake of perfecting his art. (TRAIT #6) To thank the prior, Michelangelo carved a beautiful wooden crucifix and gave it to him.

In 1494, Michelango made a small statue of St. John the Baptist for one of de' Medici's cousins, also named Lorenzo, but nicknamed *Popolano*, which means "Junior." Popolano asked Michelangelo to make it look as if the statue had been buried for some time, so he could pass it off as an artifact and sell it for a higher price. The artist, intrigued by the caper and perhaps wondering if he could pull it off, agreed. But he and Popolano were both cheated out of their fee by a middleman. As soon as the Cardinal who bought the sculpture realized it was a fake, he was so impressed by the talent of the actual artist that he invited Michelangelo to Rome.

He arrived in Rome at the age of twenty-one. Within a year, the French ambassador to the Vatican commissioned one of Michelangelo's most loved works, the *Pietà*, a sculpture of the body of Jesus after crucifixion, held by his mother, Mary.

The sculpture took two years to create. When it was first put on public display, the artist proudly stood close to listen to the crowd's reaction. It was an immediate sensation. (TRAIT #5) As Michelangelo's first biographer, Vasari, put it, "It is certainly a miracle that a formless

---

TRAIT #6 - I have the courage to take risks

block of stone could ever have been reduced to a perfection that nature is scarcely able to create in the flesh."[8]

But Michelangelo overheard one visitor say to another that it was clearly the work of a different, more famous sculptor. Enraged, that night after the crowds left, Michelangelo went to work on the sculpture with his chisel, and carved the words, "Michelangelo Buonarroti, Florentine, made this" into Mary's sash. He later regretted this prideful act, and swore he would never again sign one of his works.

Now, in 1504, with the statue of David completed, Michelangelo was lavished with praise and nicknamed Il Divino ("the Divine One"). The great Leonardo da Vinci, in his fifties, had recently returned to Florence, to his usual acclaim. But as attention shifted to Michelangelo, da Vinci grew angry at this usurper. The hostility between the two artists became the stuff of legend.

Michelangelo returned to Rome on the invitation of the new Pope, Julius II. The Pope wanted to commission Michelangelo to paint the ceiling of the Sistine chapel. More sculptor than painter, the artist was reluctant to take on the job, but the Pope insisted and Michelangelo had to accept.

The original commission called for a fairly simple design: the twelve Apostles against a starry sky. Driven by his ardent religious faith, he insisted on a far more ambitious design, one that represented Creation, the Downfall of Man, the Prophets, and Salvation. (TRAIT #9)

---

[8] Giorgio Vasari, *Lives of the Artists*

TRAIT #5 - I delight in sharing what I do

Michelangelo designed his own scaffold, a flat wooden platform that was supported from holes in the wall rather than rising from the floor (in order to save on the cost of wood). (TRAIT #4) He painted standing up (not flat on his back, as popular imagination has it). He used fresco, with the paint applied daily, directly to wet plaster. Instead of using a large paper pattern (called a *cartoon*), as was common at the time in fresco, he drew his compositions freehand, directly on the ceiling. And he innovated freely, beginning with a wash to lay down broad areas of color, then as those dried he went back to add shade and detail.

He worked on the ceiling from 1508 to 1512. The painting ultimately included nearly 350 figures and several events from *Genesis*. He did not enjoy the process, as he wrote in his journal, "After four tortured years...I felt as old and as weary as Jeremiah. I was only 37, yet friends did not recognize the old man I had become." (TRAIT #8)

Unveiled in August 1511, the ceiling impressed all who saw it, especially the other artists of the time. Raphael, who did not expect much from Michelangelo's efforts at fresco (at which Raphael himself excelled), was so moved by the work that he actually changed his own style in response.

In 1523, Michelangelo expanded his repertoire to architecture. He designed the Laurentian Library in Florence, part of the church of San Lorenzo. Many of his choices were engineering innovations, including his new style of columns and use of space. (TRAIT #12)

When the citizens of Florence overthrew their rulers four years later, there was a siege of the city. Michelangelo was asked to aid Florence

TRAIT #4 - I merge my left brain and my right brain; TRAIT #8 - I persevere;
TRAIT # 12 - I shape the future

by preparing the city's fortifications. He ingeniously protected the bell tower of one church by completely covering it with mattresses.

In 1532, at the age of fifty-seven, Michelangelo met the young nobleman, Tommaso dei Cavalieri, and he was smitten. Although it's unclear if they ever had a physical relationship, Michelangelo addressed a large number of his three hundred love sonnets and madrigals to him. (TRAIT #11)

This caused a great deal of consternation to Michelangelo's descendants. When these love letters were first published in 1623 by the artist's great-nephew, the gender of masculine pronouns were intentionally changed to feminine to make it seem the artist was writing to a woman. Similarly, early art historians (and some today) have done their best to portray these clearly erotic poems as Platonic paeans to friendship.

The artist was commissioned to paint the fresco of the Last Judgment on the Sistine Chapel's altar wall. When he completed it in 1541, the naked figures of Christ and the Virgin Mary caused a scandal. Although the Pope defended the work during Michelangelo's life, after his death their genitals were painted over. Michelangelo's work was often subject to censorship, and the first use of a "fig leaf" was on this work.

Around the time he was painting the altar wall, Michelangelo fell in love with the widow Vittoria Colonna. They exchanged letters and spent years conversing, but their relationship remained chaste, even as Michelangelo wrote her love poems. After she died, Michelangelo

---

TRAIT #11 - I challenge the status quo

claimed his only regret in his long life was that he did not kiss her face with the same passion he had kissed her hand.[9]

Near the end of his life, Michelangelo was made chief architect of St. Peter's Basilica in the Vatican, and was charged with designing part of the building and its dome. Although he was well into his 70s, exhausted and ill, he accepted the job as he felt he had been called upon by God to do it. He completely revised the earlier plan that had been developed, and construction of the famous basilica began. He knew he would never live to see it completed, but his only hope to realize his vision, he felt, was to get the construction far enough along before he died or fell from exhaustion, so that his design could not be changed. (TRAIT #10)

He died in Rome at the age of eighty-eight, and at his request his body was brought to Florence to be buried. This great Renaissance Man who pushed himself relentlessly to greater and greater heights said: "I hope that I may always desire more than I can accomplish."

---

[9] Ascanio Condivi, *The Life of Michelangelo*

TRAIT #10 - I have vision

# Galileo Galilei

## (1564 - 1642)

*Expert in astronomy, physics, mathematics, philosophy; improved the telescope
and the compass, discovered four of Jupiter's moons and the phases of Venus;
supported heliocentrism, the then-heretical theory that the sun is the center of our
solar system; author of several books of new sciences; studied and taught fine arts.*

(TRAIT #1)

Early one morning in 1633, while the Italian hillside was a
checkerboard of dark and light greens, the silent façade of a stone
building in the heart of Rome hid the dramatic confrontation taking
place within.

As torchlight flickered in the great hall, the rapid interplay of
light and shadow on walls may have, on another occasion, fascinated
Galileo. But now the old man's head was bowed as he kneeled before
the six Cardinals of the Inquisition.

---

TRAIT #1 - I am outstanding in my field and exceptional in many areas

Galileo had been called to Rome to answer to the charge of heresy for the views he had presented in his 1632 book, *Dialogue Concerning the Two Chief World Systems*. Within its pages, he had brought up the banned concept of *heliocentrism*—the notion that the Sun is the center of our solar system, and that Earth revolves around it. Galileo had been aware of the thin ice he was on, having been warned some years earlier by that same Inquisition not to discuss the concept except as a "mathematical fiction." So he had been cautious: before he had written a single word, he had sought official permission from the Inquisition to write the book, and he hadn't presented the idea as a literal fact but as part of a theoretical debate.

But in the end it made no difference. Because here he was, summoned before the Inquisition anyway! Galileo knew he risked confinement and torture unless he recanted. Just a few years earlier a man who expressed the same heretical notion—that Earth traveled around the Sun—had been burnt at the stake. So the risk was real. How had he gotten to this place?

Galileo Galilei was born in Pisa, the son of a lute player and composer. As a young man, he learned to play the lute himself, and was considering joining holy orders when his father convinced him to study medicine, a very highly paid profession at the time.

At the University of Pisa, however, Galileo found a different passion. Inspired, perhaps, by the chandeliers he watched swing back and forth at the school (maybe when he found the lectures particularly dull), he set up experiments at home using pendulums, to time their sweeps. (TRAIT #2) Around the same time, he inadvertently entered the

_____

TRAIT #2 - I am insatiably curious

wrong lecture hall and found himself in a geometry lecture, where he fell in love with mathematics. He pleaded with his father to let him change his area of study from medicine (with a high earning potential) to math and science (and an uncertain income). (TRAIT #9)

Although his father relented, Galileo did not have an easy time of it—he had a sharp tongue and dry wit, and he would ridicule those at the university he disagreed with. He earned himself the nickname, *il litigante*, or "the wrangler"[10] (in the sense of one involved in a long and complex quarrel), and he left Pisa without a degree.

For a time, Galileo, who had spent some time studying fine art, became an instructor at a school of art and design in Florence, where he focused on teaching perspective and chiaroscuro, the effect of light and shadow in a drawing or painting.

Then, at the age of twenty-two, his book, *The Little Balance*, described his invention of a new kind of scale. (TRAIT #7) This brought him to the attention of the academic world. Especially striking was the way Galileo combined scientific theory and practice, which differentiated his work from that of his peers,[11] and at twenty-five he was offered a chair in mathematics at Pisa. (TRAIT #3)

Around this time, the story goes, Galileo dropped two lead weights, one large and one small, from Pisa's famed Leaning Tower, to test Aristotle's axiom that heavy objects fall faster than lighter ones. The experiment, supposedly witnessed by several students and faculty, proved Aristotle wrong when both the heavier and lighter weights

---

[10] Isaac Asimov, *Asimov's Biographical Encyclopedia of Science & Technology*, Doubleday 1982
[11] The Galileo Project, "Hydrostatic Balance" at http://galileo.rice.edu/sci/instruments/balance.html

TRAIT #3 - I embrace culture; TRAIT #7 - I create; TRAIT #9 - I am passionate

landed on the ground at exactly the same moment. (The only problem with this tale: neither Galileo nor anyone else wrote about the incident at the time. Most scholars today conclude this was just a thought experiment on his part, not a test he actually conducted.)

When his father died some years later, Galileo took over the care of his younger brother, a frequently unemployed lute player who was constantly borrowing money from Galileo. This put stress on Galileo's finances, until he found a way to increase his income. In 1595 he designed an improved military compass that would help artillerymen aim and fire their canons faster. He designed a civilian version for surveyors soon after. With the income these generated, he could pay off both his sisters' dowries and provide his younger brother with some needed spending money.

Then, in 1609, the world changed—nearly literally—for Galileo and, well, the world. He heard of an invention called a "spyglass," invented in the Netherlands. Within twenty-four hours, Galileo had built his own with 3x magnification, and within a year he had developed an improved device with 30x magnification. The term "telescope" was coined in reference to Galileo's invention, and he was actually able to make some money with it—an important consideration for Galileo—by selling them to merchants who used them at sea or traded them.

Up until then, spyglasses were used to observe distant points on Earth. Galileo was the first man known to point his to the heavens, and he published what he saw there. His 1610 book, *The Starry Messenger,* proclaimed his discovery of the four moons of Jupiter—now called Io, Europa, Ganymede and Callisto (TRAIT #5). The notion that celestial

---

TRAIT #5 - I delight in sharing what I do

objects were revolving around another planet upended the belief that all such objects must revolve around Earth, (TRAIT #11) although several scholars and religious authorities of the time flatly refused to believe it.

When Galileo viewed the moon through his telescope, thanks to his artistic knowledge of chiaroscuro he immediately understood that the light and dark patches he saw there were caused by mountains and craters (TRAIT #4). Up until then, authorities had insisted the celestial bodies were perfectly smooth.

Galileo also observed the phases of Venus, which could only be explained if the planet were traveling around the sun—another notion believed not only impossible, but heretical.

In 1616, Galileo made his first appearance before the Inquisition—a voluntary one—to plead his case for heliocentrism. He claimed nothing he had observed or written about contradicted the Bible. He quoted St. Augustine, who suggested that some of the more poetic passages in the Bible should not be taken literally.

Although the Inquisition wasn't moved by this argument, they basically let Galileo off with a warning. They ruled that Earth *is* the Center of the Universe, and that Galileo should not question the authority of the church. However, they gave him permission to discuss heliocentrism as a paradoxical notion, a "mathematical fiction," as it were, but warned him not to present it as a literal fact. For many years, Galileo avoided the subject altogether.

Still, this did not inhibit his continual and avid explorations of science and scientific principles. (TRAIT #8) In his 1618 book, *The*

---

TRAIT #4 - I merge my left brain and my right brain; TRAIT #8 - I persevere; TRAIT #11 - I challenge the status quo

*Assayer*, Galileo explored the nature of science itself. He described how he believed science should be studied, with experiments to confirm theories with the help of mathematics. In this book, he wrote the famous line, "Mathematics is the language in which God has written the universe." Many scholars consider the work his manifesto.

At some point, Galileo discovered he could use his telescope to make small nearby objects look larger, and in 1625 he modified his device for that purpose. While he called it "the little eye," his device was later dubbed the "microscope."

Finally, in 1632, he could no longer hold back his heliocentric theories. (TRAIT #6) He conceived of his book as a dialogue, with each speaker defending his own position, and heliocentrism as just one theory. Perhaps he went too far when he made the defender of the Earth-centered universe appear quite foolish. Perhaps he shouldn't have had this fool (whom he named "Simplicio") quote the arguments of Pope Urban VIII, who upon reading it, viewed the work as a personal attack.

No matter. Because now he was, quite involuntarily this time, before the Inquisition, awaiting his fate.

Maybe because of his fame, or the frailty of age, the punishment, when it was announced, was relatively light. Galileo was told if he recanted his heliocentric view, he would be allowed to live out the rest of his days under house arrest.

Galileo was no martyr. He bowed his head and recited a formal statement: "I have been judged vehemently suspect of heresy, of having held and believed that the sun is the center of the universe and immoveable, and that Earth is not at the center of same..." The statement culminated in a full recantation of his beliefs.

---

TRAIT #6 - I have the courage to take risks

According to a legend first told long after his death, when Galileo finished uttering the official statement, under his breath he muttered, "And yet, it moves." It's a pretty story, but in reality, Galileo, by then an old man, may have just counted himself lucky to escape with his life.

His controversial book was banned, and Galileo returned to his home, which he was not allowed to leave, save for medical emergency, until the day he died. While there he wrote what many consider his finest book, *Dialogue Concerning Two New Sciences*. It was smuggled out of Italy and published in Holland.

That book summed up his studies and advances in the two sciences now called kinematics and material mechanics. His studies in motion foreshadowed the classical mechanics of Newton, and he even postulated a basic principle of Einstein's relativity. (TRAIT #10)

For these and his other contributions to the scientific revolution, especially the necessity for experimentation and the importance of mathematics to science, (TRAIT #12) Galileo has been called the Father of Modern Science.

In Albert Einstein's book, Ideas and Opinions, he wrote, "Propositions arrived at by purely logical means are completely empty as regards reality. Because Galileo realized this, and particularly because he drummed it into the scientific world, he is the father of modern physics—indeed, of modern science altogether."[12]

---

[12] Albert Einstein, (1954). *Ideas and Opinions.* translated by Sonja Bargmann. London: Crown Publishers.

TRAIT #10 - I have vision; TRAIT # 12 - I shape the future

# Blaise Pascal

---

## (1623 - 1662)

*Mathematician, physicist, author and religious philosopher; inventor of the first mechanical calculator and roulette wheel.* (TRAIT #1)

Blaise Pascal flicked the reins in his hand and the horses pulling his carriage galloped faster. He had taken the four-in-hand out many times, on nights when he craved raw horsepower. Even now, as he gave them their lead for a few paces, he enjoyed the roar of their hooves, like a storm on the horizon.

It was the night of November 23rd 1654. He had been vacationing in Neuilly-sur-Seine, but pressing matters were calling him back to the manor he had inherited from his father. He'd been administering the estate since his father's death three years earlier.

---

TRAIT #1 - I am outstanding in my field and exceptional in many areas

He remembered the day when, as a child, his father, a provincial judge, had brought young Blaise and his sisters to Paris because of the boy's precociousness in science and mathematics.

This was somewhat ironic, Blaise mused, because when he was little, he was only allowed to study languages at first, not math or science, as his parents were concerned that his constitution was weak. Then he discovered math by himself, fell in love with it, (TRAIT #9) and discovered many mathematical properties and propositions on his own.[13] (TRAIT # 2) By the age of fourteen, he was invited to attend weekly meetings of prominent French mathematicians, a group which later became the French Academy. (TRAIT #3)

When Blaise was a lad of sixteen, he developed a new mathematical proof regarding hexagons inscribed in conic sections. He was so confident about his idea that he sent the paper to Père Mersenneone, (TRAIT #5) one of the age's pioneers in mathematics, who was duly impressed. (That proof is still known as "Pascal's Theorem.")

In 1639, his father had been appointed tax commissioner for Rouen. Thanks to the constant social turmoil in the city, Rouen's tax records were a mess. Blaise was concerned about the long hours his father spent doing addition and subtraction. To ease his father's burden somewhat, the young Pascal, still a teenager, invented the world's first mechanical calculator. (TRAIT #7)

Unfortunately for the family's financial well-being, the machine, dubbed the *Pascaline*, was not a commercial success. The machines, hand built with many moving parts, were too expensive for most

---

[13] W.W. Rouse Ball, *A Short Account of the History of Mathematics* (4th edition, 1908) via http://www.maths.tcd.ie/pub/HistMath/People/Pascal/RouseBall/RB_Pascal.html

---

TRAIT #2 - I am insatiably curious; TRAIT #3 - I embrace culture;
TRAIT #5 - I delight in sharing what I do; TRAIT #7 - I create; TRAIT #9 - I am passionate

people. But Pascal continued to improve the design, and it paved the way for later advances.

As he devoted more time to science, Pascal began to focus on hydraulics, pressure and vacuums. He not only invented a hydraulic press (using the pressure of fluids to increase force), but he also invented the syringe. His experiments with liquid in a barrel—extending a thin tube up to the third floor of a building in order to fill the barrel to bursting, thereby proving that pressure is related to the elevation of a fluid rather than its weight—became legendary.

His quest to produce a vacuum (using tubes filled with mercury, then called "quicksilver") led to years of debate with other scientists who argued (based on the writings of Aristotle) that actual vacuums did not exist. (TRAIT #11) In defense of his results, Pascal wrote one of the most important early papers describing the scientific method.

Then, while trying to create a perpetual motion machine, Pascal invented an early roulette wheel and introduced that game of chance to the world. He was also the first person in recorded history to wear a wristwatch—by tying his pocket watch to his wrist!

Blaise's horses' hooves thundered on the roadway, the wheels creaked in the crisp night air, as his carriage roared onto the bridge. He recalled the moment when his father had broken his hip, and the elder Pascal allowed only two doctors in France to treat him. As it happened, both were adherents of a form of Catholicism known as Jansenism – an Augustinian-based doctrine that accepted predestination, and taught that divine grace, rather than good works, was the key to salvation.

Over the course of treating his father they had long conversations with Blaise. He was greatly influenced by these talks, and for a time he

TRAIT #11 - I challenge the status quo

stopped pursuing math and science to focus on theological writing. He spent two years in religious studies, immersing himself in the single-minded contemplation of "the greatness and the misery of man,"[14] as he put it later in the Pensées. (TRAIT #8)

Pascal was drawn back to worldly affairs when his father died and he took over the administration of his estate. Over the next two years, he developed more original ideas in mathematics. First he developed what became known as "Pascal's Triangle," an elegant presentation of algebraic properties. Then, prompted by a friend who proposed a curious math puzzle involving gambling, Pascal began a correspondence with Fermat over this question which led to the development of the theory of probability. (TRAIT #10)

But now, as his carriage approached the middle of the wooden bridge, gambling took on a whole new meaning. Something—he was never sure what—spooked the lead horses. Suddenly they were galloping out of control—he pulled on the reins but they slipped from his hands as the carriage approached the edge. To Pascal's horror, the two lead horses plunged over the side of the bridge. And then, miraculously, the traces—the leather straps connecting the horses to the carriage—broke, and Pascal was spared.

Why had God chosen him to survive, he wondered in a daze. What were the odds? Perhaps this was a sign from heaven that he was on the wrong path.

Once he arrived at his father's estate, Pascal, shaken to the core, wrote of his religious vision, using his own words and snatches of Bible verses. He ended the document with the words "I will not forget

---

[14] Ball

---

TRAIT #8 - I persevere; TRAIT #10 - I have vision

thy word, amen," from Psalm 119. (He sewed this document into the lining of his coat, and always made sure to move it to whatever coat he was wearing. The piece, now known as The Memorial, was only discovered by chance after his death, by a servant.)

After this epiphany he laid aside once again his interest in science and math, took up a simpler life, and wrote strictly about religion and philosophy. In his book, the *Provincial Letters,* published under a pseudonym, he decried the ethics of the Catholics of his day who relied on a sort of 17th century moral relativism to justify sinful behavior. (TRAIT #6) Enraged, Louis XIV ordered all copies of the book be burned.

The book remained popular, however—using humor, outright mockery and satire, it influenced the later writings of Voltaire, Rousseau, and other social satirists. (TRAIT #12)

When his deeply religious sister, Jacqueline, died in 1661, Pascal felt this was a sign to take a step back from religion. One night, he found some relief from a toothache when he turned to studying geometry—which he took as a sign that God approved of him returning to science. His last great invention was the first public bus line, which consisted of a carriage in Paris that would stop at designated stations to pick up passengers.

Pascal's other great work of literature, *Pensées* (literally, "thoughts"), was published after his death. It was presented as a dialogue between the 16th century author Montaigne, representing the philosophy of skepticism (the belief that certainty in anything is impossible), and Epictetus, the ancient Greek philosopher, representing stoicism (which

---

TRAIT #6 - I have the courage to take risks; TRAIT # 12 - I shape the future

taught that virtue is based on knowledge). As their differences seemed irreconcilable, Pascal suggested that it was not just in the analytical realms of logical philosophy or science that all answers can be found, but that one must also rely on a more intuitive sense. (TRAIT #4) For Pascal, that sense was faith, and to resolve the conflict, he felt the reader could only turn to God.

Near the end of the *Pensées*, he describes the grand gamble of life and death, which became known as Pascal's Wager. He demonstrates that it's a safer bet to believe in God than not, because the reward if God exists and one is a believer (eternal life and happiness) is greater than the loss (basically nothing) if God is not real. Or, as he put it, "If you win, you win everything; if you lose, you lose nothing."

Blaise Pascal, a man of so many extraordinary mathematical and scientific gifts was also a deep thinker for whom the meaning of life was a worthy and noble search. "For after all, what is man in nature?" he wrote. "A nothing in relation to infinity, all in relation to nothing, a central point between nothing and all and infinitely far from understanding either."[15]

---

[15] Blaise Pascal, Pensées #72

---

TRAIT #4 - I merge my left brain and my right brain

# Isaac Newton

## (1642 - 1727)

*Physicist, mathematician, author, astronomer, alchemist,*
*theologian; professor at Trinity College, Cambridge; member*
*of Parliament, Master of the Royal Mint* (TRAIT #1)

The year was 1687. Isaac Newton had been working on his masterwork, the *Principia*, for two years, and now it was published.

Strange that it all began, over twenty years earlier, in August 1665, with an outbreak of the bubonic plague. The plague, also called the Black Death, occurred near Cambridge, England. It was decided the colleges there be closed until it was safe once again for groups of young men to congregate in large enclosed rooms. Perhaps, some students thought, this is how the world ends, not with a bang, but with a whimper and bloody sputum.

---

TRAIT #1 - I am outstanding in my field and exceptional in many areas

The students were handed their degrees and sent on their way.

Among them was the young Isaac Newton, a twenty-three year old undistinguished undergrad. What his teachers didn't know was that while he endured their droning lectures on Aristotle and Euclid during the day, he stayed up until late at night in his room, studying the top philosophers and scientists of his time: Descartes, Hobbes, Galileo. He absorbed their insights, considered their theories, pored over their discoveries.

The availability of books at the school was intoxicating to him, and nothing could keep him from seeking out the newest ideas about the way our world works. (TRAIT #2) In the process Newton taught himself advanced mathematics and all the then-known sciences (for all the good it did him at school).

It wasn't that he didn't appreciate his time in college. He knew he was there only because some had seen academic promise in him. Newton's family had little money, so he had been admitted into Trinity College at Cambridge on a work-study program: he cleaned the rooms of wealthier students and waited tables in order to attend.

Isaac Newton was born in the year that Galileo had died. Isaac's own father, a farmer, had died three months earlier. The boy's mother remarried, but young Isaac never got along with his stepfather and he resented his mother for marrying him. While at Trinity, his stepfather died, and his mother pulled him out of school to try to make a farmer of him. But Isaac hated farming. He made it clear to her that that was not to be his profession, and he returned to college.

Now, as Newton journeyed back home to Lincolnshire with his degree in hand, he recalled how, at the age of twelve, he was sent to

TRAIT #2 - I am insatiably curious

King's School in Grantham.[16] While there, he lived with the local apothecary, and was fascinated by the rare earths and chemicals in glass jars and bottles, the contents of dozens of drawers and cabinets, and the tools of the apothecary's trade. He proved adept at the mortar and pestle, a skill that would serve him well in later years.

Arriving home at Lincolnshire, without the pressure of schoolwork or parental interference, Newton had the time he needed to ponder the latest discoveries and theories he had been studying. And it was there, while resting in his family's apple orchard, that he had his famous *aha!* moment. While some consider it apocryphal, the event actually occurred, as he told several people about the incident during his lifetime, including William Stukeley, an archeologist and friend of Isaac Newton.

As Stukeley wrote, many years later, the two were relaxing one day under the shade of some apple trees. Over tea, Newton told Stukeley about the time when, as a young man home from college, "the notion of gravitation came into his mind...occasioned by the fall of an apple as he sat in a contemplative mood."

The concept of gravity was not unknown at the time—Galileo had, of course, done thought experiments regarding the property (cf. the Leaning Tower of Pisa). But when Newton saw the apple fall, Stukeley wrote, he thought, "Why should that apple always descend perpendicularly to the ground? Why should it not go sideways, or upwards? But constantly to the earth's centre? There must be a drawing power in matter.... If matter thus draws matter, it must be in proportion

---

[16] It is said that Newton carved his signature in a windowsill at the school, a work of vandalism still visible there.

to its quantity. Therefore the apple draws the earth as well as the earth draws the apple."[17]

Newton's key insight was not the simple existence of gravity, but to realize that Earth's gravitational field doesn't stop at the height of an apple tree, but may also be the thing that holds the moon in orbit. As Stukeley put it, "[B]y degrees, he began to apply this property of gravitation to the motion of the earth and of the heavenly bodies: to consider their distances, their magnitudes, and their periodical revolutions…this property, conjointly with a progressive motion impressed on them in the beginning…kept the planets from falling upon one another, or dropping all together into one center, and thus he unfolded the Universe. This was the birth of those amazing discoveries, whereby he built philosophy on a solid foundation, to the astonishment of all Europe."[18] (TRAIT #10)

And so, over the eighteen months at home following his graduation, Newton undertook the most fruitful period of his intellectual life. He developed his idea of universal gravitation, the notion that the same force that applies to apples and people applies to planets and stars. He also realized the mathematics of the day was insufficient to calculate the movement of planets, (TRAIT #11) and began work on a new math that he called "fluxions" (which later became calculus). During the same period, he also developed a new theory of light and color.

In 1667, Cambridge reopened at last and Newton returned to Trinity College as a fellow. As such, he was required to become an

---

[17] William Stukeley, "Memoirs of Sir Isaac Newton's Life," 1752, MS/14, Royal Society Library, London
[18] Stukeley

---

TRAIT #10 - I have vision; TRAIT #11 - I challenge the status quo

ordained priest. Although religious, his views were unconventional—at that time of religious intolerance he would have been viewed as a radical, or even a heretic. So he postponed this requirement. When, in 1669, he was named the Lucasian Professor of Mathematics at Trinity College, a prestigious post, he could postpone ordination no longer. So Newton petitioned the king, Charles II, to waive the requirement for him—and, fortunately for both him and science, the king granted the waiver. (TRAIT #6)

In 1670, Newton began lecturing on his new theory of light: that white light is composed of all the colors of the rainbow. Then he proved it to his colleagues through an experiment, passing a ray of white sunlight through a prism, separating it into a spectrum. A second prism held up to any single colored ray would not break it into any further colors, but a prism that collected all the colored rays fused them back into pure white light.

In studying optics, Newton knew that the telescopes of his day, which used a lens to gather and focus light, were far from perfect. A lens, like a prism, spreads the different colors of light, causing the magnified images to appear somewhat fuzzy. (This effect, called "chromatic aberration," may be familiar to digital photography enthusiasts of today). In 1668 Newton solved the problem by inventing the world's first reflecting telescope. Instead of a lens to focus the light, his new telescope used a mirror which he ground himself out of an alloy of

---

TRAIT #5 - I delight in sharing what I do; TRAIT #6 - I have the courage to take risks

copper and tin. In 1671 he demonstrated his invention for the Royal Society, (TRAIT #5) and was subsequently invited to join.

In 1679, Newton's mother died, and for a time he withdrew from society. He threw himself into studies of alchemy and the occult, wherein he sought to unlock the secrets of nature. He spent much time trying to produce the "Philosopher's Stone," the ethereal substance that could turn lead to gold, and, perhaps, provide the elixir of life which would impart eternal youth. (Years later, John Maynard Keynes, the British economist, acquired many of Newton's alchemical writings, and noted, "Newton was not the first of the age of reason: He was the last of the magicians."[19]) In fact, at the time, chemistry was in its infancy and there was not much distinction between that science and alchemy. (Newton remained devoted to the study of alchemy for the rest of his life, and his theological and alchemical writings far surpassed the number of words he devoted to science and math.)

In the 1680s, the leading scientists of the day were struggling to understand the motion of planets as none of them could quite work out the math. Edmund Halley (of Halley's Comet fame, and who later became the Astronomer Royal), met Newton at a coffeehouse in Cambridge. Halley asked if he had any thoughts on the type of curve described by a planet's orbit. Newton answered without hesitation: it took the form of an ellipse. Halley professed surprise and doubt, and Newton explained that he had already worked out a proof. Halley was floored, and asked to see it. Newton, as was his custom, couldn't find

---

[19] Keynes, John Maynard (1972). "Newton, The Man". *The Collected Writings of John Maynard Keynes Volume X.*

the work among his disorganized papers, so he promised to write it out anew for Halley and send it to him.

Newton's several pages so impressed Halley that the astronomer requested a more detailed work which he would pay to have published. Newton spent nearly two years on this project, so enthusiastic he occasionally went without food or sleep. (TRAIT #9)

And now it was 1687, and his great work, called (in English) *The Mathematical Principals of Natural Philosophy*, or *The Principia* for short was published and would soon revolutionize the field of science. In the book, Newton not only included his calculation of the orbit of planets, but calculated the speed of sound, used the Latin word *gravitas* (weight), which later became "gravity," and threw in his three universal laws of motion which, among other things, set the stage for the industrial revolution. (TRAIT #12)

Although, in this book, Newton sought to explain the workings of the universe, he believed he saw evidence of conscious design in the "wonderful uniformity in the planetary system."[20] He felt he was simply explaining a universe designed by God, who created rational principles which could be discovered by any who cared to look.

Newton's fame spread internationally, but he did have his critics. Many scientists had a hard time believing an invisible force could exert influence across millions of miles of empty space—gravity seemed to them more "magick" than science, and these critics accused Newton of polluting science by invoking the alchemical belief in "action at a distance."

[20] Newton, *Opticks*

TRAIT #9 - I am passionate; TRAIT #12 - I shape the future

Then, not long after Newton's *Principia*, controversy arose over who had first invented the calculus. A few years earlier, the German philosopher and mathematician Gottfried Wilhelm Leibniz had published a book about his new developments in math which he called calculus. Newton's fluxions, which he had begun devising in 1666, shared many of the same principles, although it used a completely different notation system and he had never published the work. (TRAIT #7) Soon charges and counter-charges of plagiarism and fraud flew back and forth, charges which did not end even with Leibniz's death. Most scholars today agree that both men independently developed the new field of math.

In 1696, Newton was appointed Warden of the Royal Mint, and a few years later he became Master of the Mint, a position he held for the last thirty years of his life. It was not a full-time position, but he took his duties seriously. (TRAIT #4) He helped move the British Pound Sterling from the silver to the gold standard, and he prosecuted many counterfeiters—a crime then considered high treason. (He determined that 20% of British coins in 1696 were counterfeit.)

While he conducted his experiments on color and light at the age of 24, he didn't publish any of this work until 1704 when he was 62, in his book *Opticks*. He explained his theories through mathematics, experimentation and recordings of careful observation. (TRAIT #8) As

---

TRAIT #4 - I merge my left brain and my right brain; TRAIT #7 - I create; TRAIT #8 - I persevere

such, the book became the model for the scientific method as we understand it today.

Newton was twice elected to Parliament representing Cambridge.[21] In 1705 he was knighted by Queen Anne, becoming Sir Isaac Newton. (TRAIT #3) He never married. He was a modest man of simple tastes, who wrote in a letter, "If I have seen further, it is by standing on the shoulders of giants." He died in his sleep in 1727 and was buried in Westminster Abbey.

Newton's discoveries, often described as depicting a "clockwork universe," would so govern the world of science, that his ideas would not be challenged until the arrival, in the 20th century, of Albert Einstein, and the general and special theories of relativity.

Not long before his death, Isaac Newton told a friend, "I do not know what I may appear to the world, but to myself I seem to have been only like a boy playing on the sea-shore, and diverting myself in now and then finding a smoother pebble or a prettier shell than ordinary, whilst the great ocean of truth lay all undiscovered before me."[22]

---

[21] His tenure there was unexceptional, however. According to most accounts, his only recorded comments were to complain of a draft and request the window be shut.

[22] Cambridge University Library, "Isaac Newton at Work," http://www.lib.cam.ac.uk/exhibitions/Footprints_of_the_Lion/introduction.html

---

TRAIT #3 - I embrace culture

# Benjamin Franklin

## (1706 - 1790)

*Printer of newspapers, books and pamphlets, publisher of the hugely popular Poor Richard's Almanack; statesman, diplomat, politician, scientist, author, philosopher, philanthropist; first U.S. Postmaster General, member of the Continental Congress, intellectual leader of the American Revolution and founding father of the United States; first U.S. Ambassador to France.* (TRAIT #1)

The wallpaper of the bathroom, an elaborate wood block print depicting a rich arabesque of flowers, butterflies and medallions, glowed in the candlelight. The velvety smooth mahogany on the chest of drawers was accented by gleaming silver handles. And the porcelain of the tub was perfectly white and smooth, without so much as a chip to mar the surface.

---

TRAIT #1- I am outstanding in my field and exceptional in many areas

Benjamin Franklin enjoyed cavorting in the tub, especially when there was a lustful French lass to cavort with. Ever since he had been named the first U.S. Ambassador to France, Franklin, 77 years old in 1783, thanked his lucky stars to be alive in such a time and place, where such pleasures were de rigueur.

After his bath, sitting in a robe in his favorite armchair in front of a roaring fireplace, thinking about how much more efficient his own Franklin stove would have been at heating the room, he knew he needed to get to sleep as tomorrow was going to be a big day. "Early to bed, early to rise" after all, was one of his own aphorisms. He cast his mind back to how he had started out as the son of a candlestick maker, the eleventh of seventeen children.

Young Ben was only allotted two years of formal schooling, which he had to leave at the age of ten. He learned the rest of what he knew on his own, thanks to his love of reading and insatiable curiosity. (TRAIT #2)

At the age of twelve he was apprenticed to his older brother, James, a printer who'd begun a newspaper, *The New-England Courant*. When Ben was sixteen, James refused to print one of his letters to the paper. Not long after, a letter appeared in their offices signed by a widow, Mrs. Silence Dogwood. Her humorous and provocative letters, which James would print as soon as they arrived, became the talk of Boston—many male readers even wrote her proposals! When James found out that his little brother Ben was the one actually penning the letters, he was furious. In response, Ben abandoned his apprenticeship and lit out for Philadelphia.

In 1727, at the age of 21, Franklin founded the *Junto*, an organization of aspiring artisans and tradesmen, who wished to improve

---

TRAIT #2 - I am insatiably curious

themselves and their community. All of its members enjoyed reading as much as Franklin, and they would eagerly share rare books with each other. (TRAIT #9) Because he still couldn't get his hands on as many books as he desired, Franklin came up with the concept of a lending library, and started the Library Company of Philadelphia, which still exists today as a vast research library with thousands of rare books and manuscripts.

In 1728, he set up his own print shop, and began publishing *The Pennsylvania Gazette,* in which he urged local reforms through pointed and satirical opinion pieces. A few years later he printed the first *Poor Richard's Almanack,* which contained folk wisdom, weather predictions, recipes, and proverbs (many of which were written by Franklin himself, such as "Be at War with your Vices, at Peace with your Neighbours, and let every New-Year find you a better Man"[23]). Franklin's wit, creativity, and sure sense of what would sell, combined to make The Almanac an instant success. (TRAIT #4) It sold thousands of copies each year, making Franklin a wealthy man.

His later inventions included a mechanical glass harmonica (for which both Beethoven and Mozart composed works), the lightning rod (protecting homes from the dire consequences of lightning strikes), the Franklin Stove and bifocal glasses. (TRAIT #7) He never patented any of his inventions because, as he wrote in his autobiography, "...as we enjoy great advantages from the inventions of others, we should be glad of an opportunity to serve others by any invention of ours; and this we should do freely and generously." (TRAIT # 5)

---

[23] Benjamin Franklin, *Poor Richard's Almanack,* 1755, via Quote Investigator, http://quoteinvestigator.com/2011/12/29/franklin-new-year/#more-3217

---

TRAIT #4 - I merge my left brain and my right brain; TRAIT #5 - I delight in sharing what I do; TRAIT #7 - I create; TRAIT #9 - I am passionate

He also popularized the 18th century version of *Pay it Forward,* writing in a letter to a friend who asked for some money, "I do not pretend to give such a sum; I only lend it to you. When you meet with another honest Man in similar distress, you must pay me by lending this sum to him; enjoining him to discharge the debt by a like operation when he shall be able."

In 1743, Franklin founded the American Philosophical Society, where scientists and scholars of the day could present and discuss the latest "useful" scientific discoveries and theories. He also began his own inquiries into the nature of electricity.

Most people know the story of Franklin's most famous experiment—flying a kite in a thunderstorm with a key attached to the string, to see if lightning was electricity. However, Franklin made no mention of the event in his writing or letters at the time, and most scholars now believe it was merely a story he told his biographer. However, he documented many of his other experiments in what he then called "electric fire," and in the process coined, among other terms, "battery," "charge," and "conductor." (TRAIT #12)

Notwithstanding his admonishment to practice moderation, Franklin was a man of great appetite, in fine food, fine wine and fine things, which he detailed in his letters. (TRAIT #3) In a letter to John Bartram, a botanist and explorer, Franklin included some soybeans and went into great detail about the making of tofu (which he referred to as Tau-fu) in China, which he described as a kind of cheese.[24] And in a letter to André Morellet, a French economist, he wrote, "Behold the

------

[24] Tori Avey, "Benjamin Franklin: A Founding Foodie," http://thehistorykitchen. com/2012/01/17/benjamin-franklin-a-founding-foodie/

------

TRAIT #3 - I embrace culture; TRAIT # 12 - I shape the future

rain which descends from heaven upon our vineyards; there it enters the roots of the vines, to be changed into wine; a constant proof that God loves us, and loves to see us happy."[25]

Still despite his occasional hedonism, Franklin devoted his life to public service. He was elected to the Pennsylvania Assembly in 1751. In 1755, during the French and Indian War, Franklin wrote a letter to the Governor on behalf of the Assembly stating, "Those who would give up essential Liberty to purchase a little temporary Safety, deserve neither Liberty nor Safety."[26]

In 1757, Franklin went to England for the first time, representing the colony of Philadelphia. He arrived with no doubt that he was a loyal British subject, and as a connoisseur he appreciated the lively culture and intellectual advantages he could not find in America. But in 1765, after America's fierce opposition to the Stamp Act (a tax imposed by the British on the colonies), Franklin courageously took a stand, and testified against it to Parliament, and they repealed the law. (TRAIT #6) After this, Franklin began to feel strongly that the American colonies should be free. He returned home in 1775, just as the Revolutionary War was beginning and was elected to the Second Continental Congress, where he served with Thomas Jefferson on the committee that drafted the Declaration of Independence. (TRAIT #10) In 1776, Franklin left for France as an ambassador to the court of the French king. There he sought to persuade the king to provide help and money in the fight for independence. (TRAIT #11) In 1778, the French agreed to help, and signed a Treaty of Alliance.

---

[25] Avey

[26] Benjamin Franklin, Pennsylvania Assembly: Reply to the Governor, Nov. 11, 1755, *Votes and Proceedings of the House of Representatives*

---

TRAIT #6 - I have the courage to take risks; TRAIT #10 - I have vision;
TRAIT #11 - I challenge the status quo

Now, here he was in 1783, five years later. The British had surrendered, and Franklin was proud to have helped, that year, to negotiate the Treaty of Paris that ended the war and granted the colonies independence.

But there would be more for the elderly statesman to do when, in 1785, Franklin returned home to America. As a delegate to the Constitutional Convention, he was one of the signers of the Constitution. He also freed all his slaves and for the rest of his life became an ardent abolitionist. (TRAIT #8)

In 1790, the great man died at the age of 84 in his adopted hometown of Philadelphia. Nearly 20,000 people attended his funeral. When he was a young man, he wrote what he wanted to be his epitaph:

"The Body of B. Franklin, Printer; Like the Cover of an old Book, Its Contents torn out, And stript of its Lettering and Gilding, Lies here, Food for Worms. But the Work shall not be wholly lost: For it will, as he believ'd, appear once more, In a new & more perfect Edition, Corrected and Amended By the Author."[27]

---

[27] Benjamin Franklin, "In His Own Words," The Library of Congress, http://www.loc.gov/exhibits/treasures/franklin-transcripts.html#61

---

TRAIT #8 - I persevere

# Thomas Jefferson

## (1743 - 1826)

*Scholar, inventor, naturalist, violinist, linguist (six languages), lawyer, scientist,*
*philosopher, architect, astronomer, archeologist, horticulturist, diplomat, statesman,*
*author of the Declaration of Independence, Governor of Virginia, Secretary of*
*State, Vice President and President of the United States* (TRAIT #1)

Thomas Jefferson raised a glass to his honored guests, James Madison and James Monroe.[28] It was 1817, and the three had repaired to Monticello at the conclusion of the ceremonial laying of the cornerstone of the University of Virginia, which had been spearheaded by Jefferson.

Jefferson held the cut crystal goblet high and considered the sparkling ruby liquid, an elegant red from Nice. He had developed

---

[28] "Top Q&A About U.VA" http://www.virginia.edu/virginia/QandAGen.html

TRAIT #1- I am outstanding in my field and exceptional in many areas

his palette three decades earlier, in the salons of Paris and the fields of Burgundy and Bordeaux.[29]

After the American Revolution had ended in 1783 in victory (for the Americans, at least), Jefferson was content to serve the new nation in a fairly minor diplomatic post in France. Soon after arriving, however, he was asked to replace Benjamin Franklin as the U.S. ambassador to France. (Or, as Jefferson himself modestly put it, "succeed" him because "no one *replaces* Benjamin Franklin.")

Along with his official duties, Jefferson spent much of his time taking in the sights of Paris, learning the language and culture of France, falling in love with the architecture (as well as a married woman), and purchasing the latest in European books, art, and scientific instruments which he shipped home to Monticello. (TRAIT #3)

Things were different when he returned home. He served an unsatisfying stint as George Washington's Secretary of State—internecine political battles did not interest him, though he was proud of the cipher wheel he invented to encode State Department messages. (TRAIT #7) When he was elected to serve a single term as Vice President, he presided over a Senate with no rules yet in place. Tapping his knowledge of the British political system, Jefferson put together a quick "Manual of Parliamentary Practice"—which Congress still uses to this day. (TRAIT #10)

Now, as Jefferson sipped his wine he, Madison and Monroe reminisced about their shared recent history. Jefferson's mind flew back to those days in Philadelphia where, at only thirty-three years, he was

---

[29] James A. Bear, Jr., "Reforming the Taste of the Country," Thomas Jefferson Memorial Foundation, 1984

---

TRAIT #3 - I embrace culture; TRAIT #7 - I create; TRAIT #10 - I have vision

assigned the task of drafting the Declaration of Independence. Jefferson took on the challenge, prepared to lay out, as he modestly wrote to a friend, "my political creed in the form of a 'Declaration &c' which I was lately directed to draw."[30]

Jefferson had spent his youth absorbing and debating the latest ideas in political philosophy, batting around such intriguing notions as the "natural rights" propounded by John Locke, and the then-radical notion that government is meant to serve the people rather than the other way around. (TRAIT #11) He was heavily influenced by his reading of the Scottish philosopher David Hume and the Frenchman Montesquieu.[31] The Declaration drafted by Jefferson synthesized and elevated these concepts, heralding a major advance in the universal recognition of human rights. (TRAIT #12)

In June 1779, as the war raged on, especially in the southern colonies, Jefferson succeeded Patrick Henry as the Governor of Virginia. There he proudly introduced the bill he had drafted, "The Virginia Act for Establishing Religious Freedom." The law reflected Jefferson's interpretation of Western European history as the story of a continent torn apart by religious intolerance, and it guaranteed people's freedom to worship as they chose. Above all, he was determined to prevent the establishment of a state-sanctioned church in Virginia and throughout the nation. (TRAIT #9)

Jefferson's tenure as Governor was far from successful—a useful reminder that even the perfect Renaissance Man isn't perfect. During his second term, with the revolutionary war ongoing, U.S. General

---

[30] Burstein and Isenberg, *Madison and Jefferson*, Random House, 2010, p.35; quoting The Papers of Thomas Jefferson, Boyd et al, ed., 1:412-13

[31] Burstein & Isenberg, p. 39-40

TRAIT #9 - I am passionate; TRAIT #11 - I challenge the status quo; TRAIT #12 - I shape the future

Benedict Arnold turned traitor and attempted to take Virginia for the British. As Arnold's forces marched on Richmond, Jefferson evacuated the government to his home at Monticello.

Influenced by classical notions of space and scale, Jefferson had designed the magnificent estate himself at the age of twenty-five, clearing the land at the top of a hill. Monticello was an architectural marvel, rich not only in design and beauty, but in innovation and functionality. (TRAIT #4)

He had long been called precocious. By the time he was nine, he was learning Greek, Latin and French. Perhaps he was so studious because he was so lonely as a child. Whatever the case, he soon was studying history, science, and literature, as well as local plant and animal life. At the College of William and Mary, his subjects were math, metaphysics, science and philosophy, and in 1767 he was admitted to the Virginia bar.

It was as a proficient musician, a maestro of the violin, that he attracted his wife, Martha, a gifted pianist. It was their mutual love of music, she later wrote, that first bonded them. She died in 1782, and Jefferson was so rent by the loss that he spent the next three weeks locked by himself in his room.

Now, lost in this memory, Jefferson was silent. To lighten the mood, Monroe complimented Jefferson on the wine. Madison commented that if Jefferson hadn't ended the whisky tax, there might now be a wine tax as well.

Jefferson laughed. When he was elected the President of the United States, besides cutting the Federal budget and putting an end to the much-hated "whiskey tax" (to the delight of drinking men

---

TRAIT #4 - I merge my left brain and my right brain

everywhere), he also made three major decisions as President that changed the direction of the nation.

First, in 1803, with the Louisiana Purchase, Jefferson doubled the size of the United States by adding all the land from the Mississippi River to the Rocky Mountains, hundreds of thousands of square miles. A war-torn France, then engaged in the Napoleonic Wars and strapped for cash, offered the Louisiana Territory to the U.S. at the fire sale price of fifteen million dollars, or approximately three cents an acre. Even though such expansion wasn't yet in the thoughts of those guiding the young country and the purchase was not authorized under the Constitution, Jefferson saw the opportunity and took it. (TRAIT #6) Even his political adversaries later acknowledged the wisdom of his choice.

Second, Jefferson commissioned an expedition headed by Captain Meriwether Lewis and William Clark, to explore the newly-purchased territory and return with a thorough account of the plants, animals, and geography of the vast new region. (TRAIT #2) Lewis & Clark were also in search of a navigable waterway to the Pacific Ocean. Although the long-sought Northwest Passage didn't materialize, the wealth of scientific and geographic information Lewis & Clark brought back, detailing the newly acquired land, led to the nation's swift westward expansion.

And third, Jefferson had always argued that the sole role of the Navy was to defend the coast of the United States. However, when U.S. merchant ships came under attack in the Atlantic and Mediterranean, Jefferson sent a fleet of warships to defend the U.S. merchants from the Barbary Pirates. He thus set the precedent that America could

TRAIT #2 - I am insatiably curious; TRAIT #6 - I have the courage to take risks

deploy her might wherever and whenever her interests were threatened. (TRAIT #8)

When his less-successful second term as President ended, Jefferson had gratefully retired from national politics and returned to remodel and rebuild Monticello based on the latest architectural advances he'd learned in France. As a farmer, he had great personal interest in the latest innovations and newest crops. He'd also spent several of his later years corresponding with his fellow Founding Father, John Adams, letters that delved into politics, philosophy, literature and more. In 1815, Jefferson sold his personal library to the U.S. government, a collection so vast it became the core of the newly established Library of Congress. (TRAIT #5) (And, instead of paying off his debts, Jefferson immediately began purchasing more books!)

By then, Jefferson had given long years of thought to institutions of higher learning. When he decided to found the University of Virginia, instead of designing the school around a church, as was the norm then, Jefferson designated a central *library.* This unique design choice emphasized the supreme importance Jefferson accorded to education. The university was financed by the public rather than the wealthy, with the goal that any citizen who sought an education could attend the school. Jefferson fashioned the curriculum himself, a model of the broad depth of learning today's Renaissance Man should well aspire to. It included languages (ancient and modern), rhetoric, history, mathematics, architecture, physics, optics, chemistry, geography, and more.[32]

---

[32] William K. Bottorff, *Thomas Jefferson*, University of Toledo, 1979

TRAIT #5 - I delight in sharing what I do; TRAIT #8 - I persevere

That night, some time after Madison and Monroe took their leave, Jefferson sat at his desk and wrote out the words he wished inscribed on his gravestone.

That gravestone sits now on a patch of grass beneath a tall oak tree, near a golden wood on the grounds of Monticello. With all of his accomplishments, these are the three he wished to be remembered for:

"Here was buried Thomas Jefferson

Author of the Declaration of American Independence

Of the Statute of Virginia for religious freedom

Father of the University of Virginia."[33]

---

[33] It must be noted that another way Jefferson wasn't a perfect man, let alone a perfect Renaissance Man was his record on slavery, which was abysmal. The man who infused the nation with the notion of human rights did not apply this same principle to the over 600 human beings he owned. A bitter contradiction. His treatment of Native American Indian tribes, which he saw mainly as an impediment to westward expansion, was no better, pushing tribes off their ancestral lands in what he saw as necessity. It is for other books to argue the whys and wherefores of Jefferson's blindness to those human rights he personally trampled, but they are more than blots on his record.

# Theodore Roosevelt

## (1858 - 1919)

*Historian, explorer, travel writer, botanist, Governor of New York, Vice President and President of the United States.* (TRAIT #1)

In 1912, Theodore Roosevelt, the newly named President of the American Historical Association, watched the audience gather at Symphony Hall in Boston. Their annual convention would kick off with his keynote lecture, "History as Literature."

Roosevelt had been reluctant to take the position with the AHA. As a former President of the United States, he was busy with other duties and obligations. Besides, as he had written in a letter to a friend, he viewed the AHA as "a preposterous little organization" full of "painstaking little pedants."[34] But the heads of the AHA felt Roosevelt's

---

[34] The Letters of Theodore Roosevelt, v. III, Harvard University Press, 1951

TRAIT #1- I am outstanding in my field and exceptional in many areas

public stature, along with his reputation as a historian, would serve the organization well.[35] Ultimately Roosevelt accepted, because he hoped he could use the position to draw attention to one of the most pressing needs he saw in America: a society united through shared history.

In fact, Roosevelt had begun his career, years earlier, as a historian His first book, published when he was only twenty-three years old, was a critical analysis of the role of naval warfare in the War of 1812. It was well reviewed if not widely read at the time, and it remains the standard history of the subject today.

In between his time in politics and public service, he wrote twenty-six books of history and biography. (TRAIT #7) His multi-volume *The Winning of the West,* as one example, published as individual books from 1889 to 1896, told the story of westward expansion from the Allegheny Mountains to the Pacific, from Daniel Boone to Zebulon Pike. It was both a popular and critical success and solidified his reputation as a scholar. The work was a landmark in two ways: first, it made the study of the West a legitimate topic for future historians; and second, unlike many histories of the day, Roosevelt included the experiences of the common man in his telling. (TRAIT #3)

Roosevelt always felt a connection to the experience of the common man, despite being born into a wealthy family, rooted in America since the 17th century.

A frail, sickly, and nearsighted child, he was tutored at home. Despite his poor eyesight, he would read eveything he could get his hands on. (TRAIT #2) As a teen he was determined to make himself stronger though a dedicated regimen of gymnastics and weightlifting. (TRAIT #8)

---

[35] Nicholas Evan Sarantakes, "Theodore Roosevelt and the American Historical Association", White House Studies, v. 6, Issue 1, Nova Science Publishers, 2006

TRAIT #2 - I am insatiably curious; TRAIT #3 - I embrace culture; TRAIT #7 - I create

As he grew older, his physical activities included hiking, horseback riding, swimming, boxing and wrestling. He entered Harvard College at eighteen, majoring first in science, but then turning to history and literature. (TRAIT #4) After graduation, he got married, and spent a year in law school before he realized he had a burning desire to serve his fellow citizens through public service. (TRAIT #9)

At the age of twenty-three, about the time his naval history was being published, Roosevelt was elected to the New York State Assembly. He held that office for three years, where he became known as a progressive reformer. His future seemed clear.

Then, on February 14, 1884, both his wife and his mother died, from different causes, on the same day. It was a burden that may have broken a lesser man, and in fact, it appeared at first to have broken him. Roosevelt dropped out of politics and moved as far as he could from his home, using some of his inheritance to purchase a cattle ranch in the badlands of the Dakota Territory.

This self-imposed exile, however, only served to make Roosevelt stronger. He embraced the outdoor life, (a passion that would follow him all through his life), becoming a big game hunter (it was a different world then) and the Deputy Sheriff of Billings County.

In 1886, Roosevelt realized he'd been gone from home for long enough. He relinquished his interest in the Dakota property and he returned to New York. There he married his childhood sweetheart and rejoined the world of politics.

Now, as Roosevelt stood backstage at the AHA convention in Boston, he was aware his presence had created the buzz the organizers had hoped for. A reporter from the Boston Globe commented that

---

TRAIT #4 - I merge my left brain and my right brain; TRAIT #8 - I persevere;
TRAIT #9 - I am passionate

Roosevelt was speaking not only as a historian, but as "a maker of history."[36]

In 1889, Roosevelt had been appointed by President Benjamin Harrison to the U.S. Civil Service Commission. In 1895, he became the Police Commissioner in New York City, where he worked to clean up corruption. And in 1897 he was named Assistant Secretary of the Navy by President McKinley. He foresaw the start of the Spanish-American War and went to Cuba as a Lt. Col. of the First U.S. Volunteer Cavalry, dubbed the Rough Riders. Roosevelt had personally recruited the members of that unit from hunters and cowboys in the west. Roosevelt led a charge uphill, on foot, in the Battle of San Juan and returned home a war hero.

In 1898, Roosevelt was elected governor of New York as a Republican. But once in office, nascent progressive that he was, he refused to do the bidding of the Republican political machine. (TRAIT #11) Rather than risk having him run for reelection and continue to defy them, the party elders had him appointed McKinley's second-term running mate. In 1900, the McKinley-Roosevelt ticket won in a landslide.

Then, in 1901, President McKinley was assassinated at the Pan-American Exposition in Buffalo, NY, and Roosevelt became President at forty-two, the youngest man ever to serve in that office.

At the convention, Roosevelt waited for his introduction, knowing the historians in attendance might be offended by his address. He was going to urge them to write for a popular audience, not just for their colleagues and peers, and write literature, not vast collections of facts

---

[36] Sarantakes

---

TRAIT #11 - I challenge the status quo

on narrow subjects for the purpose of scoring points and settling scores. As an historian himself, he had seen the focus of other scholars grow less relevant to the general public. A popular literature of American history, he felt, would help bind the nation together. As he waited to go onstage, tugging his collar to allow himself more air, he no doubt recalled his first address to Congress, in December 1901, shortly after he became President of the United States.

That speech was a forceful statement for government action in the struggle between capital and labor. The very foundations of American society were at stake, he believed, and his "Square Deal" program promised to battle industrial monopolies and trusts. (TRAIT #6) The following year, as President, he brought suit against a railroad monopoly, fought for increased pay for miners, regulated industry, obtained safer working conditions and passed laws ensuring pure food and drugs. He ended America's isolationism, leading the U.S. into world affairs, and coined the phrase "Speak softly and carry a big stick." In 1903, he was instrumental in the construction of the Panama Canal, which he felt was his Presidency's greatest accomplishment. (TRAIT #12)

In 1904 he won reelection in a landslide.

He was the first president to be sworn in on a Bible, the first to drive a car, the first to fly in an airplane, the first to appoint a Jewish cabinet member, and the first to have an African American as a dinner guest in the White House. In fact, he was the President who named the presidential mansion the White House.[37] He was also the first President to win the Nobel Peace Prize, for negotiating a successful peace in the Russo-Japanese War.

---

[37] Bob Brown, "Theodore Roosevelt Literally a Renaissance Man," *The Missoulian,* October 20, 2009

TRAIT #6 - I have the courage to take risks; TRAIT # 12 - I shape the future

Roosevelt was particularly proud of his achievements in conservation. He established 150 National Forests, 51 Federal Bird Reserves, 4 National Parks, the first 18 National Monuments and more. Cumulatively, he provided federal protection for nearly 230 million acres of pristine land. (TRAIT #10)

Disappointed that the next Republican president didn't follow through with his reforms, he ran for President on the Progressive Party ticket, which was nicknamed the Bull Moose Party. Among other reforms, he pledged to inaugurate a system of national health care.

While he didn't win, Roosevelt succeeded in splitting the Republican vote, and Democrat Woodrow Wilson took the White House.

As Roosevelt strode onstage, a shout went up from members of the Progressive Party in the audience, and a number of them rose and cheered. But Roosevelt knew that if his speech were taken as a political statement, it would be ignored. So, as he spoke to the crowd of 2,500, the capacity of the hall, he made no mention of parties or politics.[38]

Roosevelt spoke of the importance of history to a nation and a people, and proclaimed historians the equal of any "immortal artist."[39] Such great writers, he stated, would be widely read and have great impact. He felt it was the civic duty of historians to follow this path, even if much of what they told about the past was unpleasant.

He stated his belief that a "soundly functioning democracy required a well-informed and educated citizenry," and that meant a

---

[38] Sarantakes
[39] Sarantakes

---

TRAIT #10 - I have vision

solid foundation in history. Roosevelt begged his fellow scholars not to forget their duty to society, and publish work accessible to fellow citizens. (TRAIT #5)

As the Boston Globe reported, he held the audience rapt for nearly two hours, his voice "seemed to grow in power and tone as he proceeded."[40] The speech was pronounced a rousing success, and an informal reception at the Copley-Plaza hotel following the event was so crowded it was moved to the hotel's ballroom.[41] Scholars and newspapermen called it "a masterpiece" and "remarkable." Henry Cabot Lodge, a historian and former Senator, and one of Roosevelt's close friends, called it one of the finest things he had ever done. His speech had a long-term impact on professional historians. While many still wrote long essays on minutia filled with convoluted sentences, many more popular histories were composed. As Allan Nevins of Columbia University put it, "Theodore Roosevelt said that history is a vivid and powerful presentation of scientific matter in literary form; and it would be difficult to improve upon this statement."[42]

[40] Boston Daily Globe, Dec. 28, 1912
[41] Sarantakes
[42] Sarantakes, quoting Ray Billington, ed., *Allan Nevins on History,* Charles Scribner's Sons, 1975

TRAIT #5 - I delight in sharing what I do

# III

## Contemporary Renaissance Men

In this section we will look at some of today's Renaissance Men. These are the icons and groundbreakers of our time. They are the innovators, game-changers and creative whirlwinds. Their presence in the world makes a difference and leaves ripples that reverberate into the future. They, like the historical Renaissance Men, have achieved mastery in a number of fields. But also like the Renaissance Men of the past, they share the other essential traits.

Their curiosity, perseverance and passion have led to inventions and technologies that have shaped the future, like the first cell phone, environmentally safe climbing equipment, a user friendly computer interface, and even a commercially produced rocket to take people and supplies into outer space.

Their understanding of their culture and recognition of its needs have enabled them to be our society's visionaries, by creating forms of sustainable transportation, re-inspiring whole communities to re-discover a way out of poverty, and introducing innovations like the iPhone that have revolutionized the technology of every day life.

Their creativity, left/right brain thinking and need to share their ideas with the world have resulted in new approaches such as combining cutting edge technology with the beauty of aesthetics, using creativity to teach businessmen how to enhance productivity, and seeking new online financial structures to reward artists for their work.

And their courage to take risks and to challenge the status quo has allowed them to promote environmental change that is also economically sound, develop a space center with the goal of multi-planetary exploration, and bring together some of the wisest leaders of our time to explore ways to solve some of the world's most pressing challenges.

There are many other ways, of course, in which the traits manifest in these men's lives. Once again we point out salient examples, although we suspect by now you've become experts at spotting them!

What is clear is that because of these shared fundamental attributes, today's Renaissance Men have grown, developed, pushed the envelope, and themselves, to accomplish the extraordinary things that they have.

We hope these stories will inspire you to look for these traits in your friends, loved ones, and most importantly, in yourself!

# Dave Stewart

---

**"It's all about connecting seemingly unconnected dots."**

*Musician, music producer, author, filmmaker, entrepreneur, corporate lecturer,*
*philanthropist; half of rock duo Eurythmics; turned Nelson Mandela's prisoner*
*number into a fundraiser; author of influential business book; foresees a digital*
*rights management revolution.* (TRAIT #1)

Dave Stewart sits back in his conference room at Weapons of Mass Entertainment, his idea factory/media shop in Hollywood, and gestures toward the poster on the wall. It appears to be "a map of the London Underground," Stewart notes, "until you look closely."

Indeed, instead of the names of subway stations, the map's colorful lines and circles show connections between disparate influence makers:

---

TRAIT #1 - I am outstanding in my field and exceptional in many areas

philosophers, scientists, actors, journalists, footballers, and more. Titled *The Great Bear*, by Simon Patterson, this London Underground map was a work of art in Charles Saatchi's somewhat controversial 1997 Royal Academy's "Sensation" exhibition in London.

"That's kind of how my brain works," he continues. "It's all about connecting seemingly unconnected dots."

Dave Stewart has been connecting seemingly unconnected dots since the beginning of his career. He is perhaps most familiar as the male half of the new wave duo Eurythmics, which he formed in the 1980s with Annie Lennox. Stewart co-wrote the gently skewed songs, produced and performed on all of them and they hit the airwaves just as MTV came into being. "Sweet Dreams (Are Made of This)" and "Here Comes the Rain Again" were two of their many hit songs. (TRAIT #7)

But Stewart has also produced numerous other recording artists, from Tom Petty & the Heartbreakers to Stevie Nicks, Mick Jagger and Aretha Franklin. The production company he founded, WME, produces music, documentaries, music videos, develops feature films and TV series, and coordinates co-ventures with non-governmental groups like Amnesty International and Greenpeace. He spearheaded a philanthropic effort on behalf of Nelson Mandela, co-wrote an influential business book, and now leads seminars for huge financial-sector corporations.

Stewart is able to meld such disparate fields by relying on both the right and left sides of his brain. Unlike many artists and businesspeople, who find it difficult to access either the logical or creative centers,

TRAIT #7 - I create

respectively, this comes easily to Stewart, but he takes no special credit for having this ability; these ideas and notions come to him unbidden.

"It has to do with fireworks in the brain," he says. "If you imagine your brain is connected like railroad tracks, there are some neurons firing on the right side, the creative side. There's something going on that you're seeing, a sort of a vision." Stewart then has the ability to connect these visions back to the left side of his brain. "Oh, I'm gonna turn this into a piece of music," he says by way of example, and then gestures toward the conference room wall, "or an Underground map of philosophers."

Even though he knows artists are not always the most business-oriented individuals ("If you're having a business meeting, you give them five minutes before they're doodling"), he sees the ability to embrace both sides of the brain as a natural, necessary one for the successful artist. "There are two worlds," he says. In music, for examples, "one is being a brilliant musician. You can compose and play and everything." But you'll be doing that alone in your bedroom, he notes, unless you can get people to hear you.

When you go back in time, Stewart points out, the great musicians, the great artists, have also been brilliant marketers. It's not an ego-driven thing, he hastens to add. "It's pragmatic, in a way. How am I gonna eat? Or how is this ever going to mean anything to me or anybody else unless it's seen or heard? It's being realistic; we're embroiled in this world. We have kids and families. Even new bands starting off, at some point are going to need a roof over their head.

"So throughout my strange journey," he goes on, "I've always had this side of the brain working," he holds his hand over the right side of his head, "and this side of my brain working," he moves his hand to the other side, "and I think what has happened is that it has slowly fused together, so now I don't even think about it." (TRAIT #4)

MTV helped launch Eurythmics, but in the early 1980s, when Stewart and Lennox were first developing their concept, they didn't even know that the new music television channel was on the horizon. Stewart was having trouble getting the record label to even share his vision over the name of the duo.

"It's a funny story actually," Stewart recalls. "Annie used to practice something called Eurhythmy," created by Swiss composer Emile Jaques-Dalcroze and developed in the early 1900s by philosopher and social reformer, Rudolf Steiner. "It was about rhythm," Stewart continues, "and getting kids aware of the beat with movement. So we liked that, because it had movement and dancing, and we liked 'Eur' at the beginning because that was like Europe." He shakes his head. "Anyway, we knew the record company wouldn't like it because it's a hard name, Eurythmics. So I went in the office with the A&R guy and the CEO, and to their shock and disbelief , I leapt from a standing position up onto the boardroom table and said, 'We are EURYTHMICS!' Sometimes you have to just do drastic things like that." The label execs were taken aback, but they went with it.

Dave Stewart learned how to do things like that in Sunderland, England, where he was born in the latter half of the 20th century. Sunderland is a seaside town where shipbuilding and coal mining, the town's two main industries, were then in steep decline, and the town's other industries, such as glassmaking, were facing stiff competition from overseas.

---

TRAIT #4 - I merge my left brain and my right brain

Dave's cousin, who had moved to Memphis, Tennessee, sent young Dave blues records, like Robert Johnson and Howlin' Wolf. He had never heard any music so rough and honest and raw. "It's why I learned to start playing the guitar. And there are elements of those records, and what I felt when I listened to those records, that still underlie everything I do." (TRAIT #9)

He'd already been in a few bands when he was introduced to Annie Lennox in the late 1970s. With a band called The Tourists, they achieved only modest success. When that band dissolved, Stewart and Lennox teamed up as a duo and Eurythmics was born.

Once Stewart convinced the label to go with the name, he wanted to come up with a strong video to promote the single both he and Annie thought was a unique sound, *Sweet Dreams*.

"I wrote down a storyboard of the video, sort of like a cartoon sketch." But the record executives looked at his sketch and just didn't get it. They had expected a conventional pop video, with the band just playing their song. But Stewart envisioned little vignettes "inspired by Buñuel" (the original surrealist) and his film *L'Age d'or*, about "the insanities of modern life."

Stewart and Annie Lennox, went about creating an iconic image. Annie cropped her hair and they both wore the same man's suit. Then, in one of his vignettes, Stewart put himself and Annie in a corporate boardroom with an actual live cow. Lennox spins a globe in front of a projection screen displaying rockets and crowds, while Stewart sits close by punching keys on an early rhythm computer terminal, as the live cow circles the conference table.

---

TRAIT #9 - I am passionate

"It was a real struggle because we were in the center of London trying to get a cow down into a basement in Soho," he laughs. Then, in the middle of editing the video, Stewart noticed the cow turned around and looked straight at the camera. He froze the image, and turned the cow purple. He laughs again and says "this was about 20 years before Seth Godin's book, *The Purple Cow.*

"I was really making a video about how crazy people have become, and how divorced they are from the world of nature and so forth. We're saying, *are* sweet dreams really made of the world we're living in?" So it was only natural that the video would juxtapose dreamlike images.

Luck and timing were on their side. As Stewart recalls, "It hit the TV in America and MTV didn't have many things to play, so they put this thing on." It was seen several times a day.

For those who don't remember its original incarnation, MTV was the first 24-hour music television network, playing three-minute rock videos all day and all night. It needed massive quantities of product.

In part because of its in-your-face imagery, the rock video of *Sweet Dreams* became an instant MTV hit, going into heavy rotation on the network. Stewart still laughs when he thinks of people throughout the U.S. watching videos of rock bands just playing their songs, "and then this thing would come on, this girl with bright orange cropped hair in a suit. And people were questioning it, like, 'Hey, is that a guy? Are we watching some kind of gender-bender thing?' It all just exploded and we ended up on the cover of Newsweek and Rolling Stone." He shakes his head at the vicissitudes of fate. "And that little idea, which is a tiny idea that's just turned left a bit instead of the road most traveled, and us inflicting that on a label and saying no, this is how it has to be, changed the whole course of our lives."

And it's a strong vision of how things should be and a commitment to creativity that has led Stewart to the choices he's made.

Before Eurythmics called it quits in 1989, Stewart had already begun producing other artists' music. He also began scoring films, including Robert Altman's *Cookie's Fortune*, and Ted Demme's *Beautiful Girls*. In 2006 he founded Weapons of Mass Entertainment, his self-described "idea factory."

Today, WME has become a successful little production company, housed in a classic Hollywood building with a traditional doorman. Gold and platinum records stretch up the walls, two stories from floor to ceiling, and awards haphazardly fill the display cases—including Grammys, Hall of Fame, a Golden Globe or two, and Critics' Choice awards. In one darkened editing suite, an editor cuts a Deadmau5 dance video shot at the Sepulveda Dam in Sherman Oaks. Three other editors are hard at work on other projects.

At any one time, Stewart says, "we have ten or twenty things going on. It's the idea factory. (TRAIT #2) I have these ideas and then I have literally a factory of people, editing and making, as one example, little short teasers of films." In May 2012, Hollywood talent agency ICM started representing WME in film, television, music, theater and new media projects.

One recent WME project that Stewart is particularly proud of is the band SuperHeavy, which features himself, Mick Jagger, soul singer Joss Stone, Indian composer and super-star A. R. Rahman, and reggae star Damien Marley.

As Mick Jagger put it, "Dave really wanted to make a record with a group of musicians with different backgrounds of music. (TRAIT #3)

---

TRAIT #2 - I am insatiably curious; TRAIT #3 - I embrace culture

Instead of everyone being a rock musician, he wanted to get as many genres together that would fit. I said it sounds like a good idea. I never thought it would actually happen."

But Stewart made sure it happened, and he couldn't be happier. "It sounds fantastic. The glue that makes it work is those seemingly unconnected dots, where one musician's playing this eastern kind of melody, and it lands here, which kicks off a bass that's from Jamaica, and then something else comes in, and something else…and in the end, you're listening to it going this is the weirdest sounding thing, but somehow it makes sense."

WME's other recent projects include two feature length documentary films now on the festival circuits, three feature films in various stages of development, and a hit ABC primetime television series that Stewart conceived of after an outing to Malibu.

"It is completely insane how my brain works. For instance I said to a couple of friends, 'Let's go to Malibu and take cowboy hats,' I don't know why. So we're all sitting around in cowboy hats and I got somebody to take some pictures and a bit of an improvised film of it. So it's kind of back to front. I'm looking at the pictures and the film clip and I'm kind of wondering what it is, and I come up with a story idea of this country singer in Nashville. She (played by Reba McEntire) gets divorced from her superstar country singer husband and moves to Malibu, on the beach. She's brought the kids and her mother (played by Lilly Tomlin) with her to start all over again."

Although Stewart is a literal rock star, he had no illusions about his less-than-iconic status within the TV world when he first pitched the concept. "When I got to present the idea, I was quite aware of people going well, hang on, this a pop musician and why is he getting into the television side. So I arrived with this…"

He holds up a beautifully crafted pine box with the name *Malibu Country* burned into the wood. The box slides smoothly open to reveal, among other trinkets, photos of the cast, a bound story synopsis/treatment and a CD of potential songs for the show. "Ha! I even had the t-shirt and hat inside the box. When you show this kind of presentation to people, it's like, do you want it or not? (TRAIT #6) I create these things," he hefts the box, "to make sure they understand, A, I know what I'm doing, and B, you can't steal it."

It worked. *Malibu Country,* starring Reba McEntire and Lilly Tomlin, premiered on ABC primetime in fall 2012 to 9.2 million viewers.

Stewart's experience in the music and television industries led him to write his book, *The Business Playground* (now in nine languages), with marketing and advertising guru, Mark Simmons. The book explores creativity and demonstrates how to link it to business using games that Stewart and Simmons developed.

"There's the CEO game, which is quite funny. How do you get your idea to the CEO? Another game is called Idea Spaghetti. I think it's much better having lots of ideas than having no ideas."

In addition to writing the book on identifying and harnessing your creativity, he began leading seminars on that very topic for large businesses—including firms like Deutsche Bank , Razorfish and Deloitte & Touche. (TRAIT #5)

Stewart understands he's perceived as swimming against the tide to cross boundaries the way he does. "A lot of people in contemporary times, they don't want you to be an engineer and a film maker. They

TRAIT #5 - I delight in sharing what I do; TRAIT #6 - I have the courage to take risks don't want you to be a musician and lead corporate seminars—they can't cope with it. (TRAIT #11)

"When I walk into a company, first, they can't get their head around it, they've put me in a box: This is a pop musician or a songwriter and now he's telling us how to change our business? But after five minutes they really get into it.

"I make them play games about their own business. And one of the things I do which is quite interesting is I say: Look, in a song, a hit song, you've got to get the idea across pretty quick, like in the opening bars. But there's this thing called a chorus and the chorus has to hit the nail on the head with what the whole thing's about, whether it's 'I can't get no satisfaction' or whatever it is. So let's do a song about your company, what is your company about?

"And there's eight hundred people sitting there. And they've all got different ideas. So I make them come up with what is the chorus, and this one company ends up deciding on, 'Always one step ahead' which they have used as their slogan ever since.

"I tell them: 'It's like I'm outside looking in at your company's website. I'm gonna stay there less than half a second unless I understand A, what it is that you are saying and B, that it is interesting enough to keep me remotely engaged .'"

As he speaks to these corporations, he uses examples from his own career, describing for instance how difficult it was for him and Annie to get their label to back their band.

"There were various decisions we made along the way that we had to hide from everybody. Like when we appeared on the Grammys, we did the sound check and we went through the run-through and John

---

TRAIT #11 - I challenge the status quo

Denver was hosting. We did it with Annie dressed normally. And then we hid in a secret location where Annie got made up with sideburns and black slicked-back hair and a man's suit and when we came on to do it for the audience she walked right past John Denver and he didn't recognize her at all. She walked up to the mike, and the whole audience was like this..." he holds his mouth agape, eyes open wide, "because this woman's voice was coming out of this guy. And suddenly there were only two people the next day all over the press, it was Michael Jackson and this weird duo from England. We'd just invaded America."

With all of the opportunities out there, Stewart considers carefully how to pick which ones to pursue. "In *The Business Playground* we have a chapter called 'Kill the Idea.' The ideas kind of live in your brain for a bit, and the ones that won't die sort of hover up there at the top, and then there's some floating around down lower." You can't pursue all of them, he points out, so you have to kill the ones that don't rise to the top. "It's like some ideas are like a puppy dog that keeps grabbing at your jeans, and you go, ok, I've got to pay attention to this one now. And there's some that I'll have had for fifteen years and I'll just pull it out of my back pocket at the right moment. And there's some that have just happened and I've got everybody working on them."

Stewart's latest idea involves the revolution he sees coming on the Digital Rights Management (DRM) front. He has met with Visa for over two years discussing a new business model and getting their assistance in structuring it. When he first met with Visa he drew them a quick sketch of his concept. They now have his framed drawing hanging on their wall.

"For twenty-four years Visa has had a system called Visa-Net, where you swipe a card and if you bought your shirt in Milan, Italy, and your bank account's in New York, it works all that and spits out, 'Yes, give him the shirt' and it settles in twenty-four or forty-eight hours."

But in the "disappearing, crumbling pillars of the old entertainment collection system" of the music industry and film industry and book publishers, an artist would sell a record and then be paid for that actual sale anywhere from nine to twenty-seven *months* later.

"And I go, well, why? And obviously, 'why' is because they like hanging on to all the money." But a new world is now possible, he says. "What people don't understand is there's a long tail, a kind of 3D long-tail of an artist."

The "long-tail" concept, popularized by Chris Anderson in a 2004 *Wired* magazine article, proposes that thanks to the Internet, companies can find success by selling highly-targeted products appealing to a small number of customers over a very long time period. The volume is smaller but the time frame is longer.

"To give you an example of what I'm talking about, are you a fan of Bob Dylan? So I'm a fan of Bob Dylan, I'm a friend of Bob Dylan, so I know he's got a barn with stuff in it that you would love to see. It could be that Bob goes to CBS, asking: 'What about my film of me and Alan Ginsberg talking poetry to each other?' But he is stuck in a record company model that I call analogue to monologue, a fixed format. So they would say 'We make these things, records, and we manufacture them and we want ten or twelve songs to go in it.' So that film doesn't fit on the thing they make.

"Now in this 3D virtual line, if you say to all Bob Dylan fans, 'Wow, just coming out, this film shot in 1966, yes or no?' They would go, 'God I'd love to see that, YES.'

"Now, what was always missing was a rights management engine, because when you press YES it has to go: Right, that was Bob Dylan and these other people, like the Alan Ginsberg estate or the director, who also need paying because they helped enable the thing." The rights management engine makes certain everyone, especially the artist, gets paid. And the huge difference that Stewart is sure of is that, one day "he's gonna get paid in 1.4 seconds." (TRAIT #10)

DRM can go even deeper, to rights the artist doesn't control. "Take Mohammad Ali, he's done lots of amazing stuff, right? But his content is everywhere. The *Thriller in Manila* rights are possibly tied to Manila television, the interview he did with the BBC in 1966 is owned by the BBC, so it's valueless at the moment to him. But if it was all put together and aggregated with the DRM engine then you'll see that Mohammad Ali Enterprises can pay Manila TV because the engine would know exactly who gets what—they get thirty-nine cents, and they get twenty-two cents. Mohammad Ali is now the Vendor as he is the aggregator and the store front to Mohammad Ali's Virtual World. So this here is a revolutionary model being built that will alter forever the way creators get reimbursed or paid up front."

His two year process with Visa resulted in a working structure for his concept. He then went to Nokia and their design team helped build a front end prototype.

He is now co-owner of a start-up company experimenting with a way to create online "shops" that are linked to every word online or even in a digital book (it already works in his e-book *The Business Playground*), so any time someone makes a purchase from one of these online shops, the author receives a micro-payment instantly. (TRAIT # 12)

"This is a kind of rights management engine in action. Say somebody's reading this amazing novel and it's talking about Moscow

TRAIT #10 - I have vision; TRAIT # 12 - I shape the future

and you go, 'Oh, I always wanted to go to Moscow.' You then just click on the word *Moscow* [in the eBook] and it's gonna come up, along with everything about Moscow, including flights. I'd rather that author get paid as well as a Travelocity or similar service, as he stimulated the reader enough to go visit that place.

"That's been my whole job, my raison d'être, for many years. What I'm trying to do is shift the whole thing round so it puts more power in the hands of the artists, making that direct-to-the-consumers connection easier and stronger, in other words getting rid of the many tollbooths that lay across the railroad tracks between consumer and creator, so enabling disintermediation. It's great, it's a kind of future creative democracy. This model should be in place whether it's a kid in Nigeria who's crazy about football and he writes a blog and he sells football shirts, or someone making a short film about beekeeping."

Stewart takes sharing very seriously. In 2002, he worked with South African President Nelson Mandela in an effort to raise global consciousness and fight against HIV/AIDS in South Africa. "Nelson Mandela called me and said he wanted to turn his prison number 46664 into a positive number, and I had the idea to make it a phone number, working all around the world with a prefix. I wrote songs with Bono and Paul McCartney, and the only way people would hear them was by dialing that phone number, and while they're listening, it's donating to his foundation.

"This became a massive responsibility to make it all happen. It took over my life for a while and everyone's around me. I had Roger Taylor from the band Queen and his wife round for dinner one night and I was explaining all of this and they immediately jumped in to help, along with Brian May and their manager. I remember going around to Richard Branson's house explaining to him about 46664 and showing him a crazy little film of Bono and me writing songs for it. Richard was immediately positive, offering his cell phone company and Virgin Airlines to help."

He recalls the experience of first working on that project with Bono. "Bono calls me at two in the morning and wakes me up, and he's talking as if it's one o'clock in the afternoon and we're in the middle of a conversation—he doesn't say 'hello, how are you.' He's just, 'I had this idea for the song.'"

So Stewart began writing a song with him at 2:30 in the morning. "I ask my wife to try to find a tape recorder. She could only find a video camera nearby so we have a film of my knee and the phone and the guitar, and you hear Bono talking and singing. But we got Bono's song idea on tape."

That night Bono suggested they go and finish it in LA. "So the next day, literally, we were in LA—no, the same day actually—because it was two in the morning in England, then we got on a plane at four in the afternoon which got into LA at seven o'clock the same day. Then we went in the studio with Dr. Dre and Bono decides we should get this choir that he heard in Africa, and then comes a great bit of manic behavior from both of us.

"We're on the top floor of the Chateau Marmont, and now we've got four or five people...we've told our wives we would be back in maybe a day and a half, now it's like 10 days later.

"Through all the chaos we end up in the Hit Factory in New York. We've got Beyoncé, we've got Oprah Winfrey and a film crew. There's about forty people including a huge meeting going on with the NFL, about what we want to happen at Super Bowl half time, all to do with Mandela. At one point Bono and I get in this freight elevator and keep pressing the button—it just has us in it—and it is going up and down, because we don't want to get off because on every floor we have created total chaos. So we're nervous but laughing hysterically as our two minds together have manifested all of this. We keep saying 'What shall we do?'

"It was one of those moments where everything you had asked for arrives at once, but we kept it together and walked out of the Hit Factory with an anthem of a song and Beyoncé came with us to South Africa to perform it. Oprah made a week's worth of shows about the situation in South Africa and also came to South Africa for the concert."

As part of the process, Stewart recalls, "I'm filming Bono who's talking on the phone to somebody in the White House, and he's singing the words of this song on the phone. This is probably to the poor secretary of, like, Bill Clinton's assistant, you know. But why not? He was connecting as many dots as he could and that's how things get done." (TRAIT #8)

In spite of the chaos of situations like these, overall Stewart feels he leads a fairly normal life, with normal rituals. "I love having picnics, I love swimming, I love holidays on the beach and all that stuff. But I'm still thinking all the time, you know, like, 'oh that could be interesting...'

"I have a vodka martini every night about eight o'clock. I have dinner with my wife and the kids play around, all my kids are musicians, and I sort of fall asleep about 11:30, or pass out. Sometimes I wake up at four in the morning with something, and I've learnt to write it down. Because if I don't write it down I won't go back to sleep."

---

TRAIT #8 - I persevere

He considers what drives him to pursue all these different directions, and comes up with a one-word answer. "Insanity. I think I'm bordering on insanity mixed with amazing excitement of it all, the idea and life itself. It's hard to explain. When I said at the beginning about fireworks, I literally do have like, if I close my eyes, I can see fireworks. And sometimes I have it if I'm lying in bed, and it's probably a sign of some kind of madness. But luckily I just manage to sort of curve it back to an idea."

But one time, he wasn't able to hold it all together, and the insanity got the upper hand: "I went into a psychiatric hospital for about four weeks and the lady was very sweet who was running the thing, and you go into group therapy and all that stuff, and it was a little bit like *One Flew Over the Cuckoo's Nest.* I was like sneaking some of the patients out, like the Jack Nicholson character. Obviously you realize, gee, I must be crazy, cause now I've got the patients in my room and we're recording under the bed, but then I was saying no, there's nothing wrong because they're really having a good time.

"But the one thing that she did say, I've got something that might be a kind of mania. You know, I do have that thing, it's like I recognize it, and I know some people who are bipolar. I could get to the point of, okay, this is really extreme thinking, but I never go to that next point where I walk through a plate glass window shouting, I am the Lord of Hellfire, or that sort of thing, which people do. It just goes to the point of, okay this is enough chaos and I'm tired."

He takes one more stab at describing the way his mind works, the way he makes decisions. "I'll tell you a good way to explain it. I'm jamming. Jamming is like three-dimensional thinking. If you're the bass player, and I'm the guitar player, and there's a drummer, and a keyboard player, and we're gonna jam together, you can't stop and say, 'Now look, I'm gonna play F sharp now, ready?' Because everybody watching will be like, what the hell is going on? It's just got to flow out. So what I'm doing is jamming, only without music, I'm jamming in my head. That's a good way I can describe it.

# John Paul DeJoria

---

**"Success Unshared is Failure"**

*Overcame homelessness to co-found John Paul Mitchell Systems, now CEO of this $1 billion a year company; founder of Patron Spirits, the world's best-selling ultra-premium tequila, and the House of Blues; initiated and sponsors Grow Appalachia, the Appalachian Community Gardening and Food Security Project - at Berea College in Kentucky.* (TRAIT #1)

When you enter the Pine Mountain Community Garden in Appalachia, the first thing you notice is row upon row of leafy green vegetables. Look closer, and you'll see how the large space is divided by chicken wire into individual plots, where neighbors have planted an impressive assortment of green beans, cabbage, sweet corn, tomatoes,

---

TRAIT #1 - I am outstanding in my field and exceptional in many areas

potatoes, broccoli, cucumbers, and pumpkins that one intern described as the size of small balloons.

This community garden was planted with the help of Grow Appalachia, a program based at Berea College in Eastern Kentucky. The garden is a statement of affirmation, of life and self-sufficiency in the heart of a region devastated by the economic downturn and pitted with abandoned coal mines.

The entire program is just one result of JP DeJoria's fundamental belief: "Success unshared is failure." (TRAIT #5)

When JP was only two years old, his father left home, leaving JP and his younger brother to be raised by their mother alone. They lived in an apartment in the working-class neighborhood of Echo Park, on the outskirts of downtown Los Angeles.

They didn't have a lot of money in those days, but JP and his brother "lived with a mom who believed in us," JP recalls with affection. "My mom told my brother and me that we could do whatever we wanted to do. That was a big one. Knowing that as a kid."

At the age of six, his mother arranged an outing that he still remembers, one that made a huge impact on the young JP, when he experienced the feeling you get in return for giving. It was around Christmas, and he took the Red Car with his mom and brother to downtown L.A. to view the beautiful window displays in the department stores. "It was different in those days. Bullocks, May Company, it was like Beverly Hills, with little trains going around in a circle and puppets."

TRAIT #5 - I delight in sharing what I do

JP recalls that his mother gave him and his brother a dime, and said, "'Boys, hold half of it each, and go give it to that guy ringing the bell with the bucket.' And I said, 'Mom, that's a lot of money.' This is like 1951, '52, and it *was* in those days. 'Why are we giving that guy a dime?' She said, "Boys, that's the Salvation Army, and they help people that are really, really needy. Remember this in life, that no matter how bad off you are, there's always someone that needs it a little more than you do. Always try and give a little bit back. Share a little bit.'

"So we went over there, put it in, and went back to my mom. And we didn't have anything, but that dime was sharing a little bit with somebody else, and that always stuck in my head. That showed me how nice it is to give. My mom was just brilliant at that."

He remembers with fondness how his mother gave him and his brother a lot of freedom, and this led to his first brush with entrepreneurship. "At 7 years old at the Variety Boys Club, my brother and I made some flower boxes for 25 cents of wood, then went out and sold them for 50 cents. We were like, oh, that's pretty cool," he remembers with a laugh.

When he was nine, he recalls an ad on the back of a comic book. "You could send away to be in the Christmas card business! They'd send you samples, and people would give you 50% up front to put their name on it. You send it in, they send you the Christmas cards, and when you deliver them, you get the other bit for yourself." And at the age off 11, he had a paper route. "Every morning, seven days a week for the L.A. Examiner. It was a big L.A. paper in those days."

He reminisces, with some fondness, "In the 1950s, to have a job, you were the coolest kid in town. Now, I didn't keep the money, nor did my brother, we gave it all to my mother so we could have a little better way of life. But we just felt so good because it was a cool thing to have a job, right?"

Early on JP learned persistence paid off. When he was in high school, and he needed a full-time job for the summer, he'd "knock on doors for two days around the whole industrial route where I grew up in downtown L.A. until someone said yes."

Thanks to his faith in himself, perhaps instilled by his mom, he was never afraid to try anything. "When you know you have the ability to do almost anything you want to do, or at least give it a try, by gosh, you give it a try. At least I did." (TRAIT #2)

When he got out of high school, he had three choices: "Go into the military, get a laboring job, or go to college." He didn't have the money for college, so he went into the Navy as a communications technician. When he got out in 1964, JP still didn't have the money to go to college, so he took a series of jobs. First he worked as a door-to-door encyclopedia salesman for *Collier's Encyclopedia.* That experience taught him a lot.

"I sold encyclopedias for three and a half years. It was all door to door. The average life of an encyclopedia salesman is three days in the field." (The rejection comes so often, the sales are so lean.) "Three days, that's it. I lasted three-and-a-half years. You learn you have to be just as enthusiastic on door number 101 as you were on the first 100 that were slammed in your face. The more you got in, then the more you could present to. The more you could present to, the more you could close. The better you got, the less amount of doors you knocked on, the more presentations you would actually close. (TRAIT #8)

---

TRAIT #2 - I am insatiably curious; TRAIT #8 - I persevere

"I'll give you one sentence on this that I love to share with people—to be successful in life, you have to be prepared for a lot of rejection. If you start out on anything, and you're prepared for a lot of rejection, you're going to succeed. If you're not prepared, it's going to just end. That's one of the biggest tips I have to remember if I start something new or unique. Be just as enthusiastic and learn to overcome that rejection, because you're going to get a lot of rejection in almost anything you do."

JP had a very clear motivation for his persistence as an encyclopedia salesman. "Why did I do it? Why did I keep on pounding on doors? Because after four or five days when I made my very first sale, I made $70. Well, in those days, 1964-65, that was a lot of money if you made that as a kid. You sell two sets, $140, wow, that was really a lot of money. Then all of a sudden your commissions go up. But you've gotta knock on a lot of doors."

It helped that he had a strong motivation to do well. "It's that I can get nice things. The harder I work, the more I can make. Maybe one day I could get a new car. Instead of having one suit, I could buy three suits. So the motivation was, you put so much in, you get so much out."

Even with his positive attitude, the encyclopedia gig didn't last, and JP held ten different jobs over the next few years. "I sold life insurance, medical equipment, photocopy machines." Then a friend advised him to go into the beauty industry.

In the early 1970s, JP began selling hair care products. After a year and a half he was running two divisions for one company. But he lost that job and two others, in part for not socializing with the other managers. "When people fire you for not being their kind of manager, it makes you want to be your own manager."[1] (TRAIT #11)

In 1980, JP teamed up with Paul Mitchell, a hair stylist he met at a trade show. They had ideas for a number of products that would save salons time and money. (TRAIT #7) With $700 between them they launched John Paul Mitchell Systems. JP used the cash to produce samples of their brainstorm: a single-application shampoo and conditioner. But since that was JP's *last* dollar, he lived out of his car on Mulholland Drive for a few months while they got the business underway. (TRAIT #6)

"That's a true story, by the way. A couple of networks didn't believe it, so they went and checked it out, spoke to people like Joanna Pettet," the actress who found him sleeping in his car. "She let me have a room in her home."

JP went knocking on salon doors. He convinced twelve hairstylists and salon owners to order their product, and that got the ball rolling. He found a distributor to take on their line, and while that didn't give them a lot of money, it was enough to pay the bills.

The tipping point for John Paul Mitchell Systems came after they had been in business for two years. "The way we knew we'd hit it big is that after two years we were able to pay our bills on time—not pay them off, but pay them on time. And we had a couple of thousand dollars left over in the bank—this was into our second year in business. Prior to that, we probably should have gone bankrupt every week. The

---

[1] Dinah Eng, "John Paul DeJoria: Adventures of a serial entrepreneur" - Fortune Magazine/ CNN Money, http://money.cnn.com/2012/04/24/smallbusiness/paul_mitchell_dejoria. fortune/index.htm

---

TRAIT #6 - I have the courage to take risks; TRAIT #7 - I create; TRAIT #11 - I challenge the status quo;

bills were always late, and we'd call them and plead and beg, and hand-deliver checks and who knows what. We'd do whatever was necessary. But that was the tipping point for me, when we were able to pay our bills on time. That's when we knew, after this huge struggle, that we were there. We were gonna make it, and make it really big.

"Our dream when we first started was to have this little business, make it to $5 million a year—this is 1980—we'd each make a couple hundred thousand dollars, and we'd have it made. Well, we passed that $5 million and we realized, hey, we can do $50 million. And then, obviously the first hundred million year was another huge tipping point, when we knew that there's no end in sight, and we'd just keep going."

John Paul Mitchell Systems now sells hair products in over 150,000 salons in scores of countries around the world.

Once JPMS was up and running, JP entered a completely different sphere of business.

He met Martin Crowley in the late 1980s. Martin was thinking about going into business buying pavers and furniture from Mexico and bringing them back to sell to Southern California architects. Since JP was building his own Malibu estate at the time, a Mediterranean-style palace on a bluff overlooking the Pacific, he was interested. One day, JP, his builder, Jack Mahoney, and Martin were sharing a bottle of Chinaco Tequila together at his house.

"And I said, well this is pretty good tequila, but while you're down there, why don't you bring back a couple bottles of what the aristocrats drink." (TRAIT #3) When Jack and Martin were in Jalisco, Mexico, they ended up in a town called Atotonilco, high in the hills along the spine

TRAIT #3 - I embrace culture

of Central Mexico. "They came across this old factory that was run by a family for three generations." They bought a couple of bottles of their tequila and brought them back for JP to try.

It may not have been what the aristocrats were drinking, but it was smoother than any tequila JP had ever tasted. It was not a big brand, and it came in simple, ordinary bottles. "Now Martin was a very sharp, resourceful guy, and in no time at all, he found and brought back this bottle from Mexico." The bottle appeared handblown with a unique, squarish shape and a bit of a crackle in the structure of the glass. It is virtually the same *Patron* bottle they now use, except JP requested it be made out of recycled glass. Then Martin suggested hiring two distillers in Mexico to make the tequila taste even smoother.

"The bottle was so cool, I told Martin I'd order one thousand cases. That's 12,000 bottles. Very expensive in those days—still pretty expensive. My thinking was this: even though it costs three times what any tequila cost in those days, if nobody bought it, for the next ten years everybody I knew had a birthday, christening, a bar mitzvah. If you want to celebrate, I don't care how old you are, you get a bottle of tequila. So that's at least ten years worth of gifts to give away."

And then the first cases of Patron arrived. JP basically started knocking on doors again. "Martin and I would go from bar to bar. I went to the ones I knew, and he went to the ones he knew. We went to friends and said, 'Hey, here it is, what do you think?' And they said, 'Wow, that's pretty good.'" JP and Martin asked everyone they knew to turn their friends onto it, including Wolfgang Puck. "And all of a sudden it was like an underground movement."

At this point, a big distributor told them that the most they would ever sell was 20,000 cases a year. "The distributor told us, 'Your stuff is great, you're just too expensive, and we know you can't lower your price, so you'll sell maybe 20,000 cases a year.' Well, we didn't believe that."

JP was right. The company grew and grew. Now they are the number one tequila company in the world, and in 2011 alone they sold nearly two-and-a-half-million cases.

JP becomes a bit more philosophical when discussing how to choose which opportunities to pursue. "If it's of interest to me, why not pursue it? Because you know you can. I also try and pay attention to the vital few, and ignore the trivial many. If I paid attention to every single thing, I'd be a workaholic. Day and night, it'd be Paul Mitchell, Paul Mitchell, Paul Mitchell. So you learn along the way how to pay attention to the vital few, so you can do a lot more. It just happens.

"I do fewer newer things than I did before, and once they're rolling, you get great people. You need that ability to recognize people that are smarter than you and let them have the job. Don't let your ego kill you. There are so many sharp guys that will never hire anyone as sharp or sharper than they are. You've got to get people who do certain things better than you can, and if you can do that, you can move out and expand.

"And be happy at what you do. If the train's a bad one, get off."

JP recalls one story that represents one of the first times, a few years after he found success with John Paul Mitchell Systems, that he was able to give back in an immediate and real way, while expecting nothing in return.

"I went to El Torito in Marina Del Rey, and I took a friend with me, and for the first time in my adult life I ordered off the left side of the menu. (The left side is what you get and the right side is how much it costs.) Man, carne asada, a big guacamole, a big margarita—I think at that time, this was the early 1980s, maybe carne asada was $9.95. And I knew I could afford it, right? Whatever I wanted, right?

"But sitting at the big table in front of me was this inner-city lady, a black woman with her back to me, a Hispanic woman across the table from her, and about a dozen kids at the table. I knew they were inner-city kids, because I come from the inner-city—the way they were dressed, holes in the shoes, whatever. And the lady held her menu up, and I could tell she was doing what I used to do, 'Let's see what do you get for $2.95, $3.95?'

"I could see it was special for them to be there, maybe it was a birthday for one of the kids, who knows, but something good.

"I don't know why, but I followed the waiter into the kitchen, and I just told him—because it just felt good, right?— I said go back there, and tell that lady to order anything she wants, but don't tell her who I am, and I'll give you a fifteen percent tip. And that was a big deal then, because if you gave a ten percent tip, that was a big deal, but fifteen, whoa, big spender.

"Now I added up everything in my mind, like, what's this going to cost, what's the worst damage they could do? A dozen kids, a couple hundred bucks, you know? And the kids aren't going to drink alcohol, right? So I said, 'Go back there, tell the lady, but don't tell her who I am.'

"I don't know why I did that, but it just felt good, because I wanted to give. I sat down, and he tells the lady, and she was just a few feet from me, and she says, 'You gotta be kidding This can't be.' And he says, 'No, it's real. And he's going to pick up the tip too. All taken care of.' And she tells the kids what's happening.

"Then she looks around the room, trying to see who's looking at her or who looks like they could be the one that did it. She stands up, and she looks straight at me, and I can see she's like, 'No, definitely not him.'

"So then she looks around the room and, with her back to me, she raises her arms up and in an angelic voice says, loudly, 'Whoever you are, God Bless You!'

"The restaurant went silent. A pretty good sized restaurant. She says, 'You have no idea what you've done for me and these children. God bless you, whoever you are, I'd love to know who you are.' The people in the restaurant are just looking at her and she sits back down.

"Goosebumps went all over my body. And I just felt really good. And the person I was with said, 'Tell her,' and I said, 'No.' So she never knew. But I walked out and I just felt incredible."

JP has made giving back an important part of his business, supporting a wide variety of existing foundations and charities, from Habitat for Humanity to Amnesty International. In 1989, JP donated live sheep to the Navajo Nation to support their ancient weaving tradition; in 1990 he began the AIDS Relief Fund for Beauty Professionals; he donated farm equipment, blankets and food to the Tarahumara tribe; in 2008 he partnered with Food4Africa to provide meals to thousands of orphans; and he is very involved in helping the homeless of Los Angeles.

And then in 2010 he began "Grow Appalachia."

"I wanted to do something really significant for the United States," he recalls. One of JPMS's Vice Presidents, Tommy Callahan, grew up in Appalachia, an area that stretches from southern New York to the northern Mississippi. "He said there are a lot of folks up there, good folks, unemployed second, third generation coal-miners, and people are really having a hard time.

"So I did a little research and found there are over 150 thousand families in the Appalachia chain, good people, on food stamps."

Unless you live there, the crisis is mostly invisible, but due to the economic collapse and the destruction of their way of life, many people in Appalachia are going hungry. While there is an epidemic of obesity, diabetes and heart disease, thanks to the paradox of the availability of cheap, fast food, it is hard to find fresh, healthy produce.

"So I checked it out a little bit and I met some of the people, and they wanted to work and do something, but they barely make it. There are weeks where they have $3. 'Do I pay the electric bill, which is only $3 because we use so little, or do I eat?' I mean it's really tough. So I said, okay, let's knock out the food. So that's where I came up with Grow Appalachia." (TRAIT #10)

A phone call from JP to Berea College in Eastern Kentucky initiated "Grow Appalachia," the Appalachian Community Gardening and Food Security Project. Berea College set up the program and he funded it.

"I asked for no outside funds. What I do is I purchase all the equipment that's necessary for farming. If there's a large place where there are 100 rows, we'll get you a good use tractor. Here's a hoe. Here are the seeds, here's the fertilizer, here's the irrigation—everything you need."

They expanded rapidly in the first two years, and now they're going into their third year. "So first it was, here's one hundred fifty thousand dollars. How can we get the best bang for the buck? Now here's a quarter of a million. Now here's a half million more. We just

---

TRAIT #10 - I have vision

kept on ratcheting it up to see will this work, and is there a feasibility in what we're doing? What can we do?

"The end result is we have twenty-two projects right now in five states. We have it in mostly eastern Kentucky, eastern Tennessee, Virginia, West Virginia, North Carolina, which is a big portion of Appalachia."

According to their website, Grow Appalachia is dedicated to helping mountain families plant a healthy future for themselves and their communities by providing skills and resources to grow sustainable, nutritious food; learning how to prepare and preserve food in a healthy way; empowering people to share their knowledge in the community; creating programs to provide food to elderly and disabled residents; and developing local farmers markets.[2] (TRAIT # 12)

The project was in two phases, JP explains. "Phase number one, feed yourself and your family and those around you. So the first plantings were enough to feed yourself, can for the winter using food jars, and then whatever excess you have, all those destitute families around you, feed them. That took everything they had. Phase number two was, once this is underway and you're able to do a little more, now sell the excess to farmer's markets, or through farmer's markets, or to grocery stores, and market some of this food you have. In other words, get into the food business."

One success story is the Henderson Settlement Farmers Market, a community of local neighbors who sell cabbage, bell peppers, zucchini, and more. Children are learning how to plant and tend vegetables, so in a few years they'll be able to keep their own gardens. As these skills

---

[2] Grow Appalachia" on PlaceStories beta website: http://ps3beta.com/project/7724

---

TRAIT #12 - I shape the future

return to the Appalachians, the people will once again become self-sufficient. On old strip mines sites and the sides of mountains, the people of Appalachia are bouncing back, stronger than ever.

"And then part of Phase Two was, if you're really successful doing that, teach others. I want everyone to teach someone else how to do it. That's how you pay it back, you teach somebody else."

This is a very important element of the program's design. Families who go through it are asked to teach these new skills to other families, to help them become self-sufficient.

For some involved in the program, working with children, teaching some as young as ten years old how to grow food, is the most satisfying experience of all. They are the future of this region.

"We now have people gardening, we have people canning and selling it over the internet."

JP remembers a time he recently visited the area. "People came in from the mountains. There must've been a hundred people there, of every age. A lady that was 92 years old brought me a quilt she made. More vegetable baskets and canned goods were given to me than I can probably eat in a year. Just unbelievable, the generosity. And they gave me letters of how it completely changed their lives, creating communities to come together, old people working out of the house now, young people are now with their parents doing events together as a family—life changes. They can feed themselves now and before they couldn't and they were worried about it. Huge life changes."

At first JP thought this was changing Appalachia, but as one of the Grow Appalachia staffers reminded him, "We're not changing Appalachia, we're rolling Appalachia back 100 years. Before the Industrial Revolution Appalachia was the most self-sufficient area in the

United States. Everyone fed themselves, made everything themselves, traded among one another. They were completely self-sufficient. And then, of course, they lost it."

Over the course of generations, families have lost the knowledge of gardening, preparing and preserving their own food, along with the sense of self-sufficiency. "One lady walked up to me and said, 'I'm fifty-seven years old, and I remember my grandma used to garden. This is the first garden I've ever had in my life.' In other words, it was all lost. Now we're bringing them back to where they were before. I created an economy."

JP gets a bit contemplative. "If you do this as part of your life," he says, glancing around his office, "you realize you've got to have a purpose. And if you find that purpose, you know you can do something to achieve that purpose, it's within. (TRAIT #9) All of a sudden you do it a little bit, and then also you realize that if you do a little, you can do a lot.

"I'm not a detail man," he goes on. "I need a detail man and an accounts man and staff around me, but if you know your purpose and you go in that direction, and you pick people along the way to be able to do the details you can make it bigger. And then you'll be able to say, 'Okay I accomplished that goal, let me go on to something else. I did that, but I can do it so much bigger.' Now your purpose has even more meaning, and it happens naturally. Something just happens within.

"I don't know what your religious beliefs are, but from my point of view, not speaking for anyone else, we're in a body. But there's something in the body that is not the physical entity. Call it the soul, the spirit, whatever you want to call it, that's in there, and when you come into this body and you have your spirit, and you realize there are

TRAIT #9 - I am passionate

things that you can do, and along the way you realize that if you do it and everyone benefits along the way.

"If people think with their mind a lot, which most people do, your limitations are your mind and what it can conceive and believe. If you let your spirit come through, and many times it comes through without you doing anything, it's amazing what comes out. (TRAIT #4)

"You know, if you're ever confused about something, don't even think about the subject. Kick back, have a little Patron. Or a lot. Just kick back a little bit and just be. And if you have the ability to just be, what comes through you is amazing."

---

TRAIT #4 - I merge my left brain and my right brain

# Frank Nuovo

---

**"The art of business."**

*Professional drummer at twelve; Design Director at BMW/DesignworksUSA;
founded and led the Nokia design organization as VP and Chief of Design;
creation and development of the Vertu brand and products; pioneered the luxury
cell phone market.* (TRAIT #1)

Frank Nuovo brings a fresh pot of coffee and a plate with cookies and biscotti out to the deck of his California Modern mansion where his guests take in the view: rolling hills spreading out below, a line of beautiful homes on a ridge surrounded by lush greenery, the splayed splash of dark blue that is the Stone Canyon Reservoir.

---

TRAIT #1 - I am outstanding in my field and exceptional in many areas

When a loud, faraway noise, the grinding sound of construction, roars over the hillside, disturbing the beauty, Nuovo apologizes. "It's not always like that here," he swears. "This is an amazing spot, you can't even hear the freeway." In Los Angeles, it's golden not to hear cars.

He grew up far from the world of traffic, in one of the most beautiful and inspiring places on earth: Monterey.

"If I needed to be inspired, all I needed to do was go sit on the rocks at Asilomar or Carmel Beach on a stormy day and watch the waves crashing," he reminisces, dipping a chocolate-covered biscotti in his coffee. "It was amazing, to feel the power and the energy and the inspiration of that. Let me put it this way—there's no other *more* beautiful place on Earth than the Central Coast of California."


Frank Nuovo is the lead designer of the best selling cell phones of all time. No, not the iPhone.

As a consultant at Designworks/USA (starting in 1989), then as Chief of Design for Nokia (starting in 1995), he led the creation of virtually all of their cell phones, including the classic 5100 series, the more functional 6110, (both of which came with colorful face plates he created so the owners could switch the color to match their mood and wardrobe[1]), and the Communicator model—which allowed people to web surf, download news and send faxes in addition to making phone calls (in 2001, no less). *The New Yorker* called Nuovo "the Henry

---

[1] Jordan Weissmann, "Death of a Ringtone," *The Atlantic*, June 16, 2012

TRAIT #7 - I create

Ford—or at least the Calvin Klein—of cellular communication."[2] (TRAIT #7)

By most accounts, Nuovo's designs laid the groundwork for the existence of the iPhone.

Nuovo was always driven to excel. He worked every day after school from the age of 10 at Marotta's clothing store in Monterey, and worked with that same family in their band as a drummer. He was a professional musician at the age of twelve, playing jazz sessions around town. At sixteen, though still in high school, he was playing with the college jazz band and performing professionally in clubs. "I had my thing," he recalls. "And it's good to have a thing." Early on, through music and performance, he became hooked on the tremendous personal reward and excitement of positive creative interaction with other passionate and creative people.

On some nights, "a Monday, Tuesday or Wednesday night, there was practically nobody in the bar. We were playing for a couple of locals that would always show up to have a drink or two." But that was okay with him, because he remembers with warmth the feeling of "interaction between the players when you're playing for yourselves."

Besides, on other nights, it was "a room full of people, or an entire theater full of people, or a huge venue—I've done all of them." And all of those experiences still evoke intense feelings. "It demonstrated what it felt like to create something that others wanted, finding what made them feel good and it all reflected positively on you—a creative high". (TRAIT #5)

---

[2] Michael Specter, "The Phone Guy," *The New Yorker*, Nov. 26, 2001

TRAIT #5 - I delight in sharing what I do

Even then he wasn't interested in playing a song the same way it had always been done. "I wanted to know *why* it was being done that way, and I wanted to know how I could take it to another level or approach it from a different perspective. It was called fusion." Nuovo and his buddies would take a particular type of music – a pop tune, say, and turn it into a Latin or jazz tune. Re-invent it. Turn it around and play it in different musical styles and formats. "We would constantly twist existing music into new forms. It was a great exploration and often done real-time without rehearsal".

He was not only a kid drummer, he first studied classical guitar at nine then experimented with bass and piano. He was also the school artist and he drew cartoons for the school paper, he was popular socially and got along well with the brainiacs and the athletes and many of his best friends were the surfers. But even with all that, "Why is it that I really dreamed of being a football star?" he laughs. "Girls, I think, but being a drummer was okay for that, too."

Then he grows a little bit serious as he remembers those football stars. "I saw the guys who were successful in high school. And then they were launched into the real world, and all of that stuff didn't matter. And that scared the hell out of me. They were such heroes of that moment, and so popular in that social setting, but for the most part it ended at the last high school football game." It showed Nuovo how important it was to explore multiple paths—and that life will likely be a constant reinvention of oneself.

Nuovo started to feel that being a drummer, playing locally, was limiting. So as high school ended for him, he decided to go toward a parallel path—art school.

What kind of person thinks it's a smart fallback plan for a musician to study to be an artist? A damn confident one.

"I decided to go to the Art Center College of Design and change my career. I was going to expand, I wanted to learn this other thing," he remembers. He wanted to "grow, and grow quickly," so he got through the program in half the usual time. He also played music in clubs to help his parents finance his living expenses in L.A.—at one point working as much as six nights a week while holding down a full course of study. (TRAIT #8)

One of his first interviews upon graduating was with Chuck Pelly's company, Designworks (later BMW/DesignworksUSA). The twenty-four year old Nuovo wore a suit and tie and carried his portfolio to the interview, which had been set up by one of his instructors. Although he didn't know it, they were looking for a chair designer for their new account: patio furniture for Samsonite. "And my graduation project was a chair."

Chuck Pelly loved his chair. "It was very 'Chuck Pelly,'" Nuovo recalls. "He loved organic shapes and forms. He just took one look at my chair and he said, 'Can you sand?' and I said, 'What?' and he said, 'Can you sand? Can you carve foam?' and I said, 'Yeah, I can sculpt,' and I showed him my book. And he said, 'Great, you're hired,' and I said, 'When do I start?' and he said, 'Can you start now? Take your tie off, roll up your sleeves, and get to work.'"

The next thing Nuovo knew, he was being sent with a team out to Samsonite headquarters in Murfreesboro, Tennessee, the geographic center of Tennessee, a small suburban town with a population of fewer than fifty thousand. "I'll never forget that while at Samsonite I

TRAIT #8 - I persevere

wanted to work over lunch and late into the evening in the prototype workshop, but the union rules wouldn't allow it. That limitation was an early shock to me about limiting a person's own drive and initiative. It's one thing to protect someone from being abused but it's another to tell them they can't work harder if they want to!"

After that project, there were many others for Designworks, from air traffic control consoles to car interiors and physical therapy machines to computers. "Right away I didn't fit the mold for a normal designer, I wasn't just waiting around for a project, I'd just have ideas. I would go to Chuck and say 'Can I help you with that presentation?' I wanted to know how the business worked." Chuck Pelly was a big inspiration to Nuovo—he demonstrated an amazing spirit of creativity and passion for design.

Nuovo became intensely curious about the design process. (TRAIT #2) "What makes design tick really? How do you get into the heart and soul of what creativity is to these clients? How do you get these guys excited? What's it all about? All of a sudden I'm out of school, and I don't just want to have marching orders—I want to lead. So I started working with Chuck on creating client proposals, understanding how you get to know the customer, how you do research on what it is that they need, their market."

This was how Nuovo learned to approach the mechanics of the design process, by fully understanding what went into it. "I wanted to do the dissection. I see that it works but *why* does it work. What's behind it? I think the whole idea is to tear it apart, and I did, and I used that very early on. The clients would come in, and I would take them on holistically. I would want to do the proposal, I'd want to design

---

TRAIT #2 - I am insatiably curious; TRAIT #4 - I merge my left brain and my right brain

the project, present the project, I wanted the whole process. (TRAIT #4) And I was able to create almost a little company inside of the firm. And that's exactly what I did with Nokia at Designworks."

In 1989, when Nuovo was twenty-eight, Nokia came in as a client. They asked Nuovo to design an in-dash car phone for a proposal to BMW.

When he first went to Art Center, Nuovo was thinking about becoming an automobile designer, but he didn't want to pigeonhole himself. So he switched to product design. "I thought if I'm a product designer, I can still go do a car, I mean what's going to stop me? A car is made up of a thousand little products. But I found out to be a car designer you had to be a closet case, somebody that absolutely did nothing but draw cars from the time that they were born. But a product designer could take on the world—get involved in just about anything from medical products to toys."

He came through with the car phone for Nokia, and realized that could be just the beginning of their relationship. "I looked into what Nokia really needed. What was the future of mobile?" He began to understand this exciting new opportunity, "and started to tear apart the features that could be in the future." Multi-part functionality, cameras in phones, projectors, gaming and music players and a host of form factors.

If there was one advantage Nuovo had, it was seeing the future of personal tech. "I put this question to Nokia while still a consultant at Designworks/USA, 'Look, this is going to go quite far, you don't have an advanced concept development program. Let me put that together for you. Let me feed you ongoing ideas in addition to what you're doing regularly. Let me look at your colors and materials and your trends around the world that can feed into this, the way lifestyles and patterns and textures and colors play into our reactions and our emotions, and let me put together an ongoing creative program for you proactively."

Nuovo changed their business relationship into what became a nine-year long retainer, based on his own desire to help drive the process. "I said, 'Let's make this happen on a regular basis, not ad hoc, because project by project you're always putting out fires." He asked them to consider "What's possible in this whole industry?"

Nuovo was asking the same question he asked as a sixteen year old drummer and as the new guy at an established design company: "Let's tear it apart and understand it." It was a lot more than Nokia was asking for, but Nuovo convinced them. (TRAIT #11) Ultimately Nuovo's own team at Nokia was responsible for bringing to market more than 250 products and accessories a year,[3] and were selling over 400 *million* units of those products a year, making Nokia the most successful mobile phone company in the world with a market share of over 38%—while Nuovo was leading design there.

"The art of business—when you truly take business to an art form, when you really understand why business works, and work it like a sculpture—that's an art form like anything else. It's understanding why something can be successful, make money, employ people, build a culture. I have as much respect for someone who can honestly do that, with integrity, without screwing people right and left—it's the art form and a passion, whether it's a business, or whether it's making food, or wine, or sculpture or a product or a service".

---

[3] Amy Wallace, "Crème de la Cell," NY Times, April 17, 2010

TRAIT #6 - I have the courage to take risks; TRAIT #11 - I challenge the status quo

"Nokia's success took legions of people to make happen. It was driven at the start by probably a dozen people. Fortunately, I was in that group, I was welcomed into that group at the right time to represent design, to build design for Nokia essentially from scratch."

It wasn't always easy. Nuovo had to take a risk. (TRAIT #6) "I was talking to a bunch of very dry Finns about 'Love at First Sight' value." At first they didn't get it. "They said 'What are you talking about? It's a technological device.'" But Nuovo told them, "'No, you're carrying it with you, you're taking it everywhere, this has to be like a trusted companion.' And if you're going to carry it with you all the time it should have that kind of special quality. We've proven time and time again, whether it was a snuff box, a cigarette box, a whiskey flask, a watch—things that you carry with you have to have an extra quality. Something to complement your own ego and personality."

When they hesitated, Nuovo was adamant. "We need to own design," he told them. "I stood up and said things that I believed in, that made everybody sort of jump back." He chuckles a bit at the memory. "I would stand up and talk like that, and it would throw a lot of the engineers off balance, because much of Nokia leadership—they're all engineers way back."

In 2000, Nuovo went on Charlie Rose's show on PBS, and publicly coined the phrase "Fashion Tech." It was the first time he had used the term outside of Nokia. "As technology becomes more personal, as you carry it with you, as it is portable and disappears, it becomes integrated into your fashion."

By "fashion tech," Nuovo means objects that you're proud of, with their own character reflecting the taste and personality of the person who carries them. "Certainly that's been happening in watches and pens for ages already and these other sort of "objects of vertu," as they're called—objects of great personal and artistic value, personal meaning, that's an object of vertu. One of my Vertu phones is in the Objects of Vertu collection at the Smithsonian Design Museum for that reason. It's an artifact. It's like the ultimate personal reflection."

His Vertu work is heavily influenced by the art deco movement. "It's very much looking back toward the finest examples to properly see forward. All of my designs find inspiration and influence in either a classic automotive, a classic watch, a classic architectural style, or even avionics." (TRAIT #3) When it comes to style, he's always found great success building and rethinking examples from the classics while also looking forward. A fountain pen or a watch can inspire a mobile phone even as the core technologies are discovered decades or more apart.

But there's more to design than that. "A truly well-thought through idea is something that has a life of its own. When I'm designing a product, if I have an idea, I'm having a conversation—an interview of sorts with myself. I think, can I justify what I just penned—again as if I were being questioned by a difficult journalist. If I can't, I start again. For me, it's not just justifying it, it's what's the poetry behind it? Is it just a nice shape? Is it just a style variation? Am I doing it because I saw it on a car or something else and it looked cool? Well, some of that is perfectly fine if that's your goal, but what else has to work? If you can, you should always give your work multiple layers of value (functionality, style, heritage, inspirational sources, etc.), then you really have something there. Now there's nothing wrong with something just happening in your brain, with walking around absorbing constantly, going wow, that would look great on a phone or a speaker or a watch. But it has to make sense. The parallels, the inspiration, the crossover must be there. It's about the romantics of design I suppose."

TRAIT #3 - I embrace culture

Led by Nuovo, Vertu was created out on its own, as a separate company and culture, aiming at an entirely different, upscale market. Owned by Nokia but completely independent, "Nuovo's Vertu vision was the only successful offshoot brand Nokia has ever created." It had plenty of funding to make it happen. "We broke even within three-to-four years, and were profitable within four years of its launch to the public." At the time of Nokia's recent sale of Vertu, it was apparent to many it was the only truly profitable and growing part of Nokia.

Vertu became famous for Nuovo's high-end phones that cost thousands to tens of thousands of dollars. Nuovo's vision was to create an "Instrument of Communication," mostly made from authentic solid materials that last for many years. Sapphire that doesn't scratch, stainless steel, Titanium and some phones machined or formed in solid gold and platinum, trimmed with the best skins, and a few bespoke versions crafted with precious jewels. Considered a sculpture, one particular one-of-a-kind phone Nuovo designed went for over $325,000.[4] World famous artisans have created special editions using Nuovo's Signature Vertu design as the foundation—including the artisans of Bucheron Paris and Mr. Kazumi Murose, a Living National Treasure of Japan.

"Nokia had an entire ecosystem of devices and a way of working that had to be supported worldwide. You can't make a change very quickly with that scenario. It took breaking out of the company and out of the company culture in order to make a unique and successful venture like Vertu. The simple story is when you're starting from scratch with nothing to lose, then you just give it your all and see what happens."

---

[4] Wallace

But it wasn't only high fashion and luxury where Nuovo and Nokia were pushing the envelope. Nuovo also foresaw the future of high tech, and was working in rough form on many of the innovations we take for granted today. In 1986, he and his team were working on concepts such as "low-power wireless," which we now know as Bluetooth. He designed an iPad-like device with a touch screen display in 1997, but it was "too much of a power draw, the screen resolution was horrible. They were too large and heavy and wi-fi was not available everywhere as it is today." All of these concepts were on their mind, but the technology wasn't there yet. Ultimately, the Nokia Internet Tablet, with a full touch screen and Nokia apps, was released four years before the iPhone and Android models. (TRAIT #10)

On the other hand, as Nuovo points out, the technology wasn't *quite* in place for the first iPhones, either. They were "horrible in terms of talk time and standby time—they were highly compromised performers, they had a low resolution camera, they were simply a horrible phone." In spite of all their flaws, though, he acknowledges they were "wondrous new objects, the Apple solution for the ecosystem clearly was based on the successful formula of the iPod and the music store. The overall concept was so compelling, it was such a sea change in terms of how you perceive living with a mobile device."

Could Nokia have seen that coming? Well they did, "and we were working on it!" Nuovo insists. In fact, Nokia owns the patents on a lot of the technology Apple uses in the iPhone, "simple things like making a phone call efficiently, messaging protocols, lots of things that happen in the phones are software solutions Nokia invented, including the first internet and qwerty keyboard phone in 1996." (TRAIT # 12) Many companies today, including Apple, have to pay Nokia a fee for every

TRAIT #10 - I have vision; TRAIT # 12 - I shape the future

phone they sell. As reported recently in the Wall Street Journal, Nuovo had in fact shown touch concepts, including the essence of a unique ecosystem, to the public back in 1999. Published widely in the press, including in Wired Magazine, were solutions identical in many ways to current touch phones including the iPhone. Prototypes were made in the following years, however most never made it to production. Nokia had other priorities which served them well while Nuovo was there. He left Nokia in 2006 to pursue Vertu and other ventures.

*The New Yorker* profile on Nuovo quoted another Nokia employee. Erik Anderson, who compared Nuovo's design sense to Vitruvius, the Roman writer, architect and engineer, whose ancient treatise stated the three foundations of architecture: "*Firmitas*—it stands. *Utilitas*—it works. *Venustas*—beauty...They are all three equal. That is what is classical. They have to be in balance."[5]

These are all key to understanding Nuovo's work at Nokia. In particular, his relationship with Vertu recalls the ancient patron system. Leonardo da Vinci and Michelangelo, Nuovo points out, had the Medicis and the Church. "The masters would develop art and objects of utility and beauty for clients. Perhaps that's a role giant multi-national corporations, and in the case of Vertu, the role wealthy customers serve now."

To make big things happen, Nuovo notes, you need a great team. Even creative leaders like Leonardo and Michelangelo had lots of people behind them and working with them, helping them to make things happen. There were many expert talents working with Nuovo, like his good friend Dr. Peter Ashall, who was the first to take on the Vertu vision with Nuovo, and Hutch Hutchison who stood with him

---

[5] Specter

in product creation for almost thirteen years. "Do you need a patron? Not to be who you are. But certainly to get things done. I could not have come anywhere near the opportunity to have as much influence as I've been able to have on design and industry, without Nokia's backing. Millions of hits in terms of people actually using a product and learning from that."

The patrons today, he muses, in addition to corporations, are the individuals who sponsor idea creation and development labs, the Paul Allens who can finance innovation and design, those who really want to make a difference in the world.

"For a while there, Nokia, whether they knew they were doing it or not, was financing a tremendous innovation studio here in Southern California: The Nokia Design Studio in Los Angeles. We were not just doing projects that would result in a product in the short term, but we were really looking out in the very long term. Nokia was happy because they were number one. We never let them down—I never let them down."

Nuovo muses on his career. While some of it was hard, for example it was truly difficult traveling millions of miles around the globe, but it was never hard work. "It's not even work—the creative process, the effort to do something is a passion. It's why you're here. It's what you're doing. (TRAIT #9) There's no separation. I've never called it work. It was a pursuit of something which really mattered to me. And it was all about creating the beautiful music, if you know what I mean.

"I think we put way too much value on IQ and test scores. I think that's one of the biggest mistakes that we make on this planet. The reality is the folks who are really making it happen, successfully, need

---

TRAIT #9 - I am passionate

to be appreciated for going for it—living it and standing up for what they believe. Way too much emphasis is put on academics for success. Steve Jobs is a great example. The folks who are so passionate about what they do, are out there. They are unstoppable with their vision and passion and drive to create a better "thing"—whatever that might be.

"If you really want to continue with your own success, it will likely be the result of a succession of self-reinventions. I've had good success in music, I was able to work with the finest players in the world, I was able to learn from not-so-great ideas and experience a tremendous amount of praise for the good creations, and once you feel that kind of encouragement, the first thing you might do to destroy yourself is accept it, think okay, I've done it.

"What you really need to do is keep going. The same creative growth I felt as a musician continued as a designer. I have also come to believe that as long as you have the capacity and will to grow, you have to push and believe you are only as good as your next thing, not your last thing."

# Richard Branson

**"The absolute key is how good you are with people."**

*Billionaire, entrepreneur, explorer, adventurer, PR genius, Knight; founder of Virgin Records, Virgin Music, Virgin Atlantic Airways, Virgin Galactic, etc.; also an environmentalist concerned about global warming and other issues of vital importance facing the globe.* (TRAIT #1)

Located just a few miles northeast of Truth Or Consequences, New Mexico, in view of distant mountains and surrounded by expanses of desert sand and scrub vegetation, stands the sprawling, four story tall Spaceport America building. With an undulating brown roof that looks like somebody plopped a giant porcini mushroom on top of it, the building houses mission control, the astronaut prep complex, and the hangar for Virgin Galactic's Spaceship II. Spaceport America, the

---

TRAIT #1 - I am outstanding in my field and exceptional in many areas

world's first private, commercial spaceport was unveiled by Sir Richard Branson in October 2011.

To properly christen the building, Branson shimmied halfway down the massive glass wall on a thin rope to join half a dozen performing aerialists. As New Mexico Governor Susana Martinez and astronaut Buzz Aldrin looked on, Branson shook a bottle of champagne then popped it open to spray the building, and took a few hearty swigs.[1]

Two months later, Branson was sitting on a panel at the Governor's Conference on Extreme Climate Risks and California's Future at the California Academy of Sciences in San Francisco, to discuss the dangers of climate change. He noted that his airlines were developing renewable jet fuels that would reduce carbon emissions, including one derived from algae. When California Governor Jerry Brown complained of the "denial and cult-like behavior" of those who won't acknowledge the reality of climate change[2] and government officials who stand in the way of increased environmental efficiency, Branson jokingly offered those officials a one-way ticket into space.[3]

Richard Branson was never a good student. As he told Chris Anderson at a TED conference in 2007, "I was dyslexic, and I had no understanding of schoolwork whatsoever. I certainly would have failed

[1] Forbes, "The World's Billionaires: Richard Branson, March 2012, http://www.forbes.com/profile/richard-branson/

[2] Margie Shafer, "Gov. Brown Hosts International Climate Conference in San Francisco" CBS San Francisco, http://sanfrancisco.cbslocal.com/2011/12/15/gov-brown-hosts-international-climate-conference-in-san-francisco/

[3] Mark Hertsgaard, "New approach to climate deniers: Launch them into space!" Grist, Dec. 17 2011, http://grist.org/climate-skeptics/2011-12-16-new-approach-to-climate-deniers-launch-them-into-space/

IQ tests. It's one of the reasons I left school when I was fifteen years old. If I'm not interested in something, I just don't grasp it."[4]

And yet, at just sixteen, (though no longer a student himself) he set up his first business, a magazine by and for students called *Student*. As he told CNN Money, he didn't launch it to make money, he started it simply because he wanted to be the editor of a magazine.[5]

Although it didn't begin as a money-making proposition, the young Branson realized in order for the magazine to stay in business (so he could continue editing it) the venture had to make a profit. So he sold $8,000 worth of ads for the first issue. "And that," he points out, "was in 1966."

A few years later Branson, then nineteen years old, was living in a London commune.[6] He began selling records by mail order, initially just to help fund his magazine, but the music side of the business became so profitable that he opened a record shop on Oxford Street in London. He called it Virgin Records because he was a "virgin" at business. Working behind the cash register himself, the first album he sold in the store was by the German electronic group Tangerine Dream.

Music was always a passion for him, and his philosophy has always been to follow your passion. Since, as he points out, most businesses fail, "If you can indulge in your passion, life will be far more interesting than if you're just working."[7] (TRAIT #9)

---

[4] TED Conversations, "Richard Branson: Life at 30,000 Feet," March 2007, http://www.ted.com/talks/richard_branson_s_life_at_30_000_feet.html
[5] Carleen Hawn, "Branson's Next Big Bet," *CNNMoney*, http://money.cnn.com/magazines/business2/business2_archive/2006/08/01/8382250/
[6] "Richard Branson.biography" http://www.biography.com/people/richard-branson-9224520
[7] Hawn

---

TRAIT #9 - I am passionate

So, taking his own advice, he built a recording studio in 1972. Artists who recorded there included the aforementioned Tangerine Dream, John Cale and another German band, Faust. A year later, he founded the Virgin Records label, to record and release music commercially (TRAIT #4). Fortunately for him, the first album they released, Mike Oldfield's *Tubular Bells,* was a smash hit which became better known as the main title theme for the movie, *The Exorcist.* Virgin Records later signed the punk rock band Sex Pistols, alternative bands Culture Club and Devo, and even the Rolling Stones.

"I think I learned early on that if you can run one company, you can really run any company," Branson explained in his 2007 TED Conversation. First, "it's all about finding the right people and inspiring those people, drawing out the best in people." And, he adds, "I love learning. I'm incredibly inquisitive. (TRAIT #2) I love taking on the status quo and trying to turn it upside down. I see life as one long learning process."

In 1978, Branson had made enough money to buy an island—an island!—located in (where else?) the British Virgin Islands. According to reports, he bought Necker Island mainly to impress a girl—and it worked. She married him.

The following year, Branson opened the upscale, modern, stylish Virgin Megastore on Oxford Street in London, while his Virgin Books began to publish music-related titles.

And on June 22, 1984, Branson launched Virgin Atlantic Airways with its first nonstop flight from London to Newark, NJ. (He simultaneously founded Virgin Cargo.) (TRAIT #11)

---

TRAIT #2 - I am insatiably curious; TRAIT #4 - I merge my left brain and my right brain; TRAIT #11 - I challenge the status quo

As he said to Conan O'Brien in 1998, he didn't set out to own an airline, but "traveling by plane is generally pretty horrendous, so we like to make it fun."[8] Interviewed by a small group of entrepreneurs on Necker Island, Branson explained that he became an entrepreneur almost by default., Like many who feel when "something is frustrating them, they can do it better themselves," he saw opportunities. Unlike most, he was inspired to act. "I don't think you can set out to become an entrepreneur," he said, "you set out to make a difference in other people's lives."[9] (TRAIT #5)

In 1986, Branson set out on a new goal: to break records. He spent three days at sea in his 72 foot powerboat, the Virgin Atlantic Challenger II, to cross the Atlantic two hours faster than the previous record set thirty years prior.[10] In 1987, he was the first to cross the Atlantic Ocean by hot air balloon, and in 1991, he was the first to cross the Pacific the same way.

He explained to Conan O'Brien that the ballooning adventures were only partly about the bragging rights of doing something no one else has done. More than that, it was "the magnificence of flying at thirty-five thousand feet, at a hundred-and-fifty miles an hour blown only by the winds, trying to circumnavigate the world."[11]

Of course, he almost died, he admits, during each of his ballooning adventures. During the Atlantic crossing, for example, the

---

[8] Late Night with Conan O'Brien, August 27, 1998, http://www.youtube.com/watch?v=5BrKiG1cUPA
[9] Piranha Marketing, interview on Necker Island, June 15, 2011, http://www.youtube.com/watch?v=tDTX5UVoDxQ
[10] BBC, On This Day, "1986: Branson beats Atlantic speed record" http://news.bbc.co.uk/onthisday/hi/dates/stories/june/29/newsid_2520000/2520929.stm
[11] Conan O'Brien

---

TRAIT #5 - I delight in sharing what I do

balloon overshot Ireland, their landing site, and was plummeting toward the sea.[12] The more experienced balloonist he was with parachuted out, leaving Branson "holding on for dear life." He almost jumped himself, but instead piloted the balloon down to the water, and then calmly stepped out of it into the Atlantic, where he was rescued by helicopters. (TRAIT #6)

Asked about the marketing value of such heroics (or stunts), Branson demurred, explaining that "The PR experts said that, as an airline owner, the last thing I should be doing is heading off in balloons and boats and crashing them into the seas."[13]

Nevertheless, he acknowledges the importance of marketing and the value of himself as CEO of the Virgin brand. "The most important thing about marketing anything is the product itself. Is it worthy of people's attention? So make absolutely certain that you've got a product that is worth going out there and shouting about. And once you've done that, the cheapest form of marketing is to use yourself to try to put the company on the map. There are a lot of chairmen of companies who refuse to use themselves, but I think for a good chairman, at least a third of their job will be getting out there and promoting their company. And if you're going to promote your company, try to get yourself on the front pages of the papers rather than a little byline in the back pages. Be ready to make a fool of yourself. Try to come up with ideas that make people smile."[14]

---

[12] Lindstron Technologies, "Trans Atlantic Crossing"
http://www.lindstrandtech.com/Trans-alantic.html
[13] TED Conversation
[14] Piranha Marketing

---

TRAIT #6 - I have the courage to take risks

As difficult as choosing not to jump out of the balloon may have been, it wasn't Branson's hardest decision. That occurred in 1992 when he had to sell Virgin Records, the "family jewelry" as he called it, to keep Virgin Airlines afloat. Between the "dirty tricks" campaign of British Airways to shut down Virgin, the rising cost of jet fuel and a global economic meltdown, Branson had no choice but to sell his record label to Thorn EMI. "There's a very thin dividing line between success and failure, and if you start a business without financial backing you're likely to get on the wrong side of that dividing line."[15] He received $1 billion for the record label and saved the airline, but he cried after signing the contract.[16] It turned out to be the right move, but it was very painful at the time. (TRAIT #8)

"The important thing is not to take failure too seriously," he explained in 2009. "Something like 80% of all small business people fail....That's a lot of people, and some people take that really badly. And they should realize that the important thing is just to learn from it, and come back and start again. An awful lot of really big multi-millionaires and billionaires have been through two or three bankrupt companies in their lives, and have learned from them, and have come back the stronger."[17]

So, in 1992, the same year that he sold his record label, Branson opened the first Virgin Megastore in the United States on Sunset Boulevard in Hollywood. Over the next few years he started Virgin Radio, Virgin Cola, Virgin Mobile and more. In 1999, he was knighted

---

[15] TED Conversation

[16] Richard Branson.biography

[17] "Richard Branson: Learning from failure"; American Express series: Inside the Entrepreneurial Mind, http://www.youtube.com/watch?v=S_3Dj5GZJNc&feature=related

TRAIT #8 - I persevere

Sir Richard Branson for his contributions to entrepreneurship, and the Virgin Group now comprises over two hundred companies around the world, in such diverse fields as travel, communication, finance, and renewable energy. (Not every company Branson started has been a success. In 1987 he launched a condom company called Mates, and in 1996 a business called Virgin Brides, specializing in bridal gowns and accessories, which failed to thrive, he explains with a smile, because they couldn't find enough customers.)

When Branson dropped out of school at fifteen, his headmaster predicted that the boy was either going to be a millionaire or go to prison, but he wasn't sure which. Branson admits he's done both—but the two times he was arrested were in the cause of freedom of speech. He mentioned venereal disease in a public service announcement to help troubled teens, and was arrested under an obscure 1889 British law prohibiting the discussion of VD in public. Later he was arrested for releasing the album *Never Mind the Bollocks, Here's the Sex Pistols.* "The police decided 'bollocks' was a rude word," he recalled with a laugh.[18] He got off, however, when he found a linguist who explained to the court that the earliest use in English of the word "bollocks" was a reference to priests.

In the 2000s, Branson became concerned with the promotion of peace and the survival of the planet. "Global Warming is a massive threat to mankind," he told the TED conference. "We are putting a lot of time and energy into coming up with alternative fuels,"[19] including one test flight that used a jet fuel derived from coconut oil.[20] At the 2006 Clinton Global Initiative in New York, he pledged

---

[18] TED Conversation
[19] TED Conversation
[20] Interview with Renee Montagne, NPR, Oct. 10, 2012

100% of the profits from all of his Virgin transportation companies (airlines and trains), estimated at approximately $3 billion, to the fight against global warming. This money would be invested in alternative fuels and sustainable power sources. "We must not be the generation responsible for irreversibly damaging the environment," Branson said at the event.[21]

In 2007, Branson and musician Peter Gabriel established an NGO (non-governmental organization) that included Nelson Mandela, Desmond Tutu, and Graça Machel (Mandela's wife), and others. Noted for their wisdom and leadership, the group was dubbed The Elders, and Branson asked them to use their intellects and experience to help solve the world's most insoluble problems, such as climate change, HIV/AIDS and crushing poverty. (TRAIT #3) The organization has set up clinics in Africa giving out free antiretroviral drugs to battle HIV, along with free TB treatment and free malaria treatment. (TRAIT # 12)

That same year, Branson flew in a Virgin Atlantic jet powered in part by an experimental bio-fuel, and he offered the Virgin Earth Challenge: a $25 million prize to encourage scientists to develop technology that will remove greenhouse gases (including $CO_2$ and methane) from the atmosphere.

In 2008, he invited some of the wealthiest and most influential people in the world—Larry Page from Google, Wikipedia's Jimmy Wales, Elon Musk of Tesla Motors, and Tony Blair, among others—to Necker Island to discuss the question: "Is the world on fire?"[22] These

---

[21] MSNBC, "Branson bets billions to curb global warming," Sept. 21, 2006, http://www.msnbc.msn.com/id/14936341/ns/world_news-world_environment/t/branson-bets-billions-curb-global-warming/#.UIupm83vxVQ

[22] Andrew Ross Sorkin, "Thinking Green While Sifting Through the Sand," New York Times, March 22, 2008

---

TRAIT #3 - I embrace culture; TRAIT # 12 - I shape the future

entrepreneurs and titans of industry considered if, in these days of rising oil prices, the solution to global climate change is by making renewable energy a profit generating industry. Branson hopes to put together a working group of business people to find "best practices" they can share with governments and multinational corporations.[23]

More convinced than ever that the solution to global crises lies in wealth creation opportunities, Branson spoke at the "Creating Climate Wealth Summit" in Sydney in 2011. Addressing the assembled business leaders, he insisted that economic growth and clean air are not mutually exclusive. "A solution to global climate change does not mean cutting back on the growth of business," he said. "It means reshaping our approach to business, and finding a new way to create wealth and preserve the planet."[24]

Asked on Necker Island about the secret of his success, he answered without hesitation. "The absolute key is how good you are with people. If you genuinely care about people, if you can surround yourself with people who are genuinely exited about what you're doing, if you can draw out the best in people, if you're good at lavishing praise and not criticizing, at inspiring your people—never use the 'I' word, you're a team, never let it center on yourself—if you can do that from day one, then you can enjoy the good times together. But there will be bad times, and your people will pull around for you, they'll work day and night to try to keep whatever it is you're creating alive and make sure it survives. The number one lesson is to be a great people person."[25]

---

[23] Sorkin

[24] AAP Video, "Richard Branson Addresses The Creating Climate Wealth Summit" July 7, 2011, http://multimedia.aapnewswire.com.au/SearchPreviewVideo.aspx?media_item_id=20110707000330171435

[25] Piranhna Marketing

The second lesson is to be a great delegator, not to "try to do everything yourself. Whatever you're spending all your day doing, try to find someone who's better than you to do that, to replace you at it, so you can go off and think about the next big picture. An entrepreneur is not a manager, an entrepreneur is someone who is great at conceiving ideas, starting ideas, building ideas, but then handing it over to really good managers to manage the businesses. (TRAIT #7) The moment you have more than one business, you can't be hands-on doing everything."[26]

Branson continues to keep busy on the big ideas. A typical week's travel schedule for him might include appointments or appearances in Haiti, Warsaw, Cairo and Mumbai.[27] He exercises every day and keeps lists: of things to do, people to call, ideas he has. In addition to readying Virgin Galactic for launch (literally) next year, he has started considering the logistics of establishing a human colony on Mars. (TRAIT #10) Naturally, he wants to be among the first to go there.

"When I'm on my death bed, I will want to feel that I made a difference to other people's lives," he muses. "It's the way I've been brought up. If I'm in the position to radically change other people's lives for the better, I should do so."[28]

---

[26] Piranhna Marketing
[27] Jack Preston, "Productivity the Richard Branson Way",
http://www.virgin.com/entrepreneur/blog/productivity-the-richard-branson-way
[28] TED Conversation

TRAIT #7 - I create; TRAIT #10 - I have vision

# Quincy Jones

---

"There are hills and valleys in our business. You find out
who you are when you get in the valleys."

*Musician, composer, arranger, conductor, record producer, record label executive;
film and TV producer; Chairman and CEO of Quincy Jones Entertainment; best
selling author.* (TRAIT #1)

In 1960, at the age of 26, Quincy Jones wrote the orchestrations
for Harold Arlen's Broadway-bound musical, *Free and Easy*. Jones, also
the show's conductor, personally selected musicians for a nineteen
piece big band, then took them to Europe with the cast and crew of
the production for a tour of the Continent. In London, according
to the plan, Sammy Davis, Jr. would join the show, and the musical

---

TRAIT #1 - I am outstanding in my field and exceptional in many areas

would ride the success of that run back to a triumphant opening on Broadway.

It didn't quite work out that way. The show closed in Paris, before they ever made it to England. The producers, with the last of their investors' money, chartered a jet to take the cast, crew and musicians back to the U.S.

The night before the flight, Jones had a meeting with the band. They were like a family. They all knew the band they had formed was something special and this was a once in a lifetime opportunity. Unanimously they agreed to stay together and tour Europe, relying on Quincy Jones to get them gigs. The next day, the chartered jet took off without them.

"I was just young and dumb enough to not know what I was doing," Jones recalled to *Ebony* magazine in 1972.[1]

To meet the band's payroll, they had to earn $4,000 a week (in 1960 dollars; about $31,500 a week in 2012.) The band got lots of gigs but never enough, and the money never came in as fast as they needed it. Jones spent eighteen months shuttling his 19 piece big band around Europe. "If I could keep them busy and moving it was better so we wouldn't have time to think, because I hadn't figured out yet how we were going to get home."[2] By the end of 1961, Jones was $60,000 in debt (almost half a million in today's dollars).

"We had the best jazz band on the planet, and yet we were literally starving. That's when I discovered that there was music, and there was

---

[1] Louie Robinson, "Quincy Jones: Man Behind the Music," *Ebony*, June 1, 1972
[2] Robinson

the music business. If I were to survive, I would have to learn the difference between the two."[3]

Mr. Jones joins us in his living room for wine and crudités. ("This is my dope," he says with a laugh, dipping a chip into freshly-made guacamole.)

Quincy Delight Jones, Jr., was born in Chicago. "In the 30s, Depression. My father was a carpenter for the most notorious gangsters in the history of America, the Jones Boys," a black gang, who ran the South Side of Chicago. "I wanted to be a gangster until I was eleven," he recalls.

"My mother was so smart you can't believe it. She spoke 12 languages, she went to the University of Boston in the 1920s, and when I was seven years old they took her away in a straitjacket. She had dementia. My brother was six. I held my hands over his eyes, because it's pretty heavy to see your mother taken away in a straightjacket."

In 1943, when Quincy was just ten years old, Al Capone took over the rackets in their part of town. Quincy's father grabbed his kids and they took a Trailways bus to get as far from Chicago as they could go: they went as far as Washington state, and landed in Bremerton, a small town near Seattle. "We [went] from the biggest ghetto in Chicago to being the only three black kids in town. It's amazing how much trouble you can get in when you don't have anything else to do,"[4] he recalled to the Academy of Achievement in 2001.

"We broke into the armory which was right across from our home. It was a recreation center right next to the army camp. We used

---

[3] The National Jazz Museum in Harlem, "The Jazz World of Quincy Jones: The Big Band Years"; April 21, 2009 http://www.jazzmuseuminharlem.org/archive.php?id=477

[4] Academy of Achievement, "The Quintessential Artist" October 28, 2000 http://www.achievement.org/autodoc/page/jon0int-1

to go in there, because our thing was breaking and entering, that's what gangsters do. We owned the place, after Chicago, man, we were the experts, you know." One night, they heard there would be an ice cream social at the base, and Quincy and his brother decided to go into the armory after it was over. "We ate a bowl of lemon meringue pie and then ate the ice cream." Then they started exploring the empty building.

Young Quincy walked into one room, and "in the dark I saw a spinet piano. I almost closed the door, when something said, 'Idiot. Go back into that room.' And I went back in there, and went over to the piano and touched the keys."

As a young child, he had never been interested in music. "I heard music all my life, I didn't know that human beings played it." But when he touched the keyboard, his life changed forever. "I felt every cell in my body say, 'This is what you do the rest of your life.' The idea of a human being making that sound. It was over."

From that day on, he stayed after school every day, and became part of the school band. "I learned to play Sousaphone, tuba, b-flat baritone, e-flat alto, French horn, trombone—so I could be with the majorettes in the marching band, trumpets were in the back, you know. And that's why I love to write for brass so much, because I played that. I was starting to hear sounds, and I was arranging from twelve years old on."

At fourteen, he started a band with his best friend, Ray Charles, who could play the piano and sing. "When Ray came to town, he had a record player, he had his own apartment, he had two suits and two girlfriends—he was like God. He was two years older, I was fourteen and he was sixteen, but he was much older because he'd been through much more." In 1947 they were paid $7.00 for their first professional gig. By the next year they were playing back-up for Billie Holiday when she toured through Seattle.

"In Seattle in the 1940s you had to play everything, from Jewish weddings and bar mitzvahs" [5] to "the white tennis clubs at seven o'clock with the white jackets on, where we played pop music. Then we put another suit on to go play the Washington Education and Social Club, which was a joke because it was a bottle club, the wildest people in the world. We played for strip teasers and everything, rhythm and blues and all that stuff. Then we'd go to the Elks Club and play jazz all night, a jam session. That was for free."

Joseph Powe, one of Quincy's neighbors at the time, had played in a dance band years earlier and still had books of musical arrangements. Jones babysat Powe's kids just so he could study those books for hours and see how the music was laid out on the page.

At just fifteen years old, Jones almost had the chance to join Lionel Hampton's big band. He had written a piece of music, *Suite for the Four Winds*. He showed it to Hampton when the bandleader was playing a Seattle club. Hampton loved the piece and asked the youngster to join the band.

"And I went and got on the bus. I didn't go to see my parents or anybody. I just got on the bus, and I thought I'm not gonna mess this up. Because the Hamp was bigger than Basie, the Duke, and Louis Armstrong. And I stayed on that bus for six hours, and everybody got on. I'm there like a little deer in the headlights, trying to be unnoticed. And she [Hampton's wife] said, 'Hamp, who's that child on the bus

---

[5] Marc Lamont Hill, "Backtalk with Quincy Jones" Black Enterprise, Sept. 2011

back there? Come here, honey. What's your name? How old are you?'
I said fifteen. She said, 'Get off the bus, go get your education, we'll
talk to you later.'"

Jones received a music scholarship to Schillinger House in Boston
(later the Berklee School of Music). To pay his way through school,
he played music at strip joints at night, where he had to lie about his
age to get the job. "When you want to, it's incredible how little money
you can make it on."[6]

He ended up leaving the school when he got a second chance to
join Lionel Hampton's band in the early 1950s. It was a decision he
never regretted. They toured nearly every city in America and Jones
recalls they once worked 71 one-night gigs in a row. "We were happy
to do it because we were getting $17.50 a night,"[7] real money in those
days. Before long he was also getting paid to write arrangements for the
band. "There were some weeks when I would write two arrangements
and work seven nights. (TRAIT #8) I was rich!"

As he recalled the process of arranging a piece of music, "It takes
you two, three nights to sit down at the blank page of score paper,
and then try to imagine that orchestra sound in your head and put
what you think it's going to sound like on that paper. And, finally
having the orchestra there, when you do the down beat—to hear that
sound—there's no experience in the world like that. Still to this day
I feel like I'm twelve years old when I bring my hand down to the
orchestra."[8] (TRAIT #9)

---

[6] Louie Robinson, "Quincy Jones: Man Behind the Music," *Ebony*, June 1, 1972
[7] Robinson
[8] Academy of Achievement

---

TRAIT #8 - I persevere; TRAIT #9 - I am passionate

Before long, he had played with such greats as Dizzy Gillespie, and arranged for Duke Ellington, Count Basie, Tommy Dorsey, and his childhood friend, Ray Charles. "When I was a young musician, I learned to shut up and listen to people like Ray Charles and Clark Terry, Billy Eckstine, Count, Duke, Dizzy Gillespie…people like that. You can't beat that kind of education from people who know what they're talking about."[9]

Touring the country wasn't easy in those days for a black band. "We hit the road and we'd get to places like Texas. This is when every place had "white" and "colored" bus stations and water fountains, all over America….Sometimes we'd see effigies—black dummies—hanging by nooses from church steeples in Texas. That's pretty heavy, on the church steeple, and they've got a black dummy, which means "Don't stop. Don't even think about coming here," and the bus kept moving.

"It's painful. It's a killer. I loved the idea of these proud, dignified black men, and I saw the older ones wounded, and it wounded me ten times as much because I couldn't stand seeing them hurt like this. I knew their mentality, their sense of humor, their wit, their intelligence and everything, totally aware of it, and I'd see people with one-tenth of this, trying to degrade them, trying to be a giant and make a midget out of them to feel bigger. I saw it over and over and over again."[10]

"There's hills and valleys in our business," Jones mused philosophically. "You find out who you are when you get in the valleys."[11]

[9] Charles L. Sanders, "Ebony Interview with Quincy Jones," *Ebony*, October 1985
[10] Academy of Achievement
[11] CNBC.com, "Q&A With Quincy Jones: Life Lessons From the Master", July 18, 2011, http://www.cnbc.com/id/43771668/Q_A_With_Quincy_Jones_Life_Lessons_From_the_Master

Then, at nineteen, Jones went to Europe with Lionel Hampton's band, and "it turned me upside down in many ways. It gave [me] some sense of perspective of past, present and future. It took the myopic conflict between just black and white in the United States and put it on another level because you saw the turmoil between the Armenians and the Turks, and the Cypriots and the Greeks, and the Swedes and the Danes, and the Koreans and the Japanese. Everybody had these hassles, and you saw it was a basic part of human nature, these conflicts. It opened my soul, it opened my mind."[12] (TRAIT #10)

He recalled Ben Webster, the great jazz saxophone player, telling him, "'Youngblood, wherever you go in the world, eat the food the people eat, listen to the music they listen to and learn thirty to forty words in every language.' You learn so much from other cultures. You really do."[13] (TRAIT #3)

In 1956, Jones turned Johnny Mathis down to put Dizzy Gillespie's band together. "You can't plan a path like that. You just let stuff happen, just follow gravity, use your instinct about what you take and what you don't take. I didn't know it was Johnny Mathis, I didn't know who the hell he was." Mathis was a San Francisco State high jumper who nearly tried out for the U.S. Olympic Team for the 1956 Australia games, but instead embarked on his music career. Jazz producer George Avakian asked Jones to write for Mathis. "And I was starving to death. And then Dizzy said, 'Would you be the music director of my band, put the guys together, write the arrangements and meet me in three months?' I said 'Damn right.'" Jones gave the Mathis contract back to Avakian, and said, "'He's a great singer, I don't think

---

[12] Academy of Achievement
[13] CNBC.com

TRAIT #3 - I embrace culture; TRAIT #10 - I have vision

he's a jazz singer, but thank you very much. But my nation has called.' Because Dizzy was like God, you know."

It was a State Department overseas trip with Dizzy Gillespie. "We toured all over the Middle East….We went to Tehran, and Dacha, Karachi, Istanbul and Damascus. It was very exciting. Some of these people had never seen western instruments before."[14] As Jones recalls, "We called it the 'kamikaze' band," because when the Cypriot students were throwing rocks at the American Embassy, the State Department said, "'Send the Gillespie band over!' After we finished the concert in Athens, they rushed the stage—I thought we were dead, but they put Dizzy on their shoulders, shouting, 'Dizzy! Dizzy!' They were so happy.

"We came back and went to the White House Correspondent's Dinner and performed for the press people. Then they sent us to Latin America after that, Ecuador and all that.

"Well Lalo Schifrin [best known for his theme to Mission: Impossible] was down there and he saw Dizzy and he freaked out, and called his whole big band together. And Astor Piazzolla was there, a very famous bandoneón player, he created the modern tango." Piazzolla told Jones about Olivier Messiaen, the composer of Quartet for the End of Time, among many works.

In 1957, Jones moved to Paris where, on Piazolla's advice, he studied with Messiaen, "and [Pierre] Boulez on Wednesday night."

While in Paris, Jones met "the greatest composition teacher on the planet,"[15] Nadia Boulanger. "She was Rumanian and Russian

---

[14] Academy of Achievement
[15] Hill

and French. And tough." She taught Aaron Copeland and Leonard Bernstein, among others.

He smiles as he remembers. "You had to audition for her, you don't just say I want to study with you, no. She asks you, 'What are the distinguishing features of a C scale?' You know, a half step between three and four, and seven and eight. She said, 'Well, how about if we start on E and come down backwards?' And that blew my mind, it was so quick. And I said, 'I never thought of that.' It comes down on the same intervals descending, and it comes on E instead of C. It blew my mind, between C and B, you know, and F and E. I couldn't believe it. So we talked and talked and talked. And she said, 'Well, it's always crazy working with jazz musicians, because from what I've heard they shack up with music first, and then they court it and marry it later.' She was so ghetto man, it was unbelievable."

They studied at her flat in Paris at first, and that summer Jones followed her to the American School at Fountainebleau.

"She put me at the end of the day. She'd bring Beaujolais, and she loved American canned peaches, so I'd go get them from the PX. I'd bring the peaches and she'd bring the Beaujolais, and after the class we'd sit and talk, and I'd play Charlie Parker for her, and all that stuff. So we became friends then. She said in a lot of her books that Stravinsky and myself were the ones she had the most fun with. She was a great lady."

Boulanger was also the mentor to Igor Stravinsky, one of the most influential composers of the 20th century, whom Jones felt fortunate to meet. "Stravinsky used to say the most important part of an artist's responsibility is to be a great observer."[16]

---

[16] Academy of Achievement

His greatest lesson from Boulanger, he says, is "Melody is king. There's rhythm, and there's harmony, and there's melody. Melody is king, and it still is."

To earn a living while he was in Paris, he went to work for Barclay Disques, Mercury Records' French subsidiary, and recorded great French artists like Charles Aznavour and Jacques Brel, along with touring Americans like Sarah Vaughn and Andy Williams.

"You don't know what's going to happen, man," he notes. "Hell no. You just keep on going."

When he returned to the U.S., he got back into the world of jazz. "Bebop was strange, you know. It came out of big bands and just morphed its way into all these other things. But the bands were on the way out, because the guys that got into bebop, Charlie Parker, Dizzy, Miles, Sarah Vaughn—Billy Eckstine took all of them over to his band, and all the bebop revolutionaries, Dexter Gordon, Kenny Clark, Miles Davis, all those guys, they went so far in the revolution that they went over the audience's head.

"Coltrane had Slonimsky's book with him every day, the Thesaurus of Scales and Melodic Patterns. That's where he got 'Giant Steps' from—you can't get away from the science of music, it's the Left and Right brain, and any kid who studies music, they learn everything quicker. Math and music are cousins. Every time you play music you're using left and right brain—emotion and science. You always use that. You cannot play music and not use both simultaneously. Every time you play. You can't get away from it." (TRAIT #4)

He sighs and shakes his head. "The standards were different then. We were not into money or fame, not even close. It was about being good and trying to revolutionize the music. We were trying to

---

TRAIT #4 - I merge my left brain and my right brain

follow Charlie Parker and those guys. They wanted to be artists, they didn't want to entertain any more. I used to watch Bird listening to Stravinsky, and he said 'I want to be that kind of artist,' you know. A real creative artist.

"And Stravinsky recognized it too, because he got into jazz. And so did Debussy and Dvořák and Bizet, all those classical composers. They never heard that sound before. Composers think like that, when something is brand new, they know it, they know it first."

Jones laughs. "Today, it's a waste of time to even give a lead sheet to anybody. They don't know what you're talking about. Chords? They think a chord is something to wrap around your neck. They don't have a clue."

In 1959, Jones went back to Europe with his own big band for that ill-fated musical, Free and Easy, which went bust in Paris, leaving him and his musicians stranded in Europe. He did all he could to keep the band working, including a thirteen city tour of the Soviet Union. (He only found out when the tour was over that the money they earned there was worthless outside of the Soviet Union.)[17]

When he finally got all the musicians home, by selling or hocking nearly everything he owned, the President of Mercury Records, a good friend of his, offered Jones a job. "I was vice president, and got a chance to really learn what the record business was all about. It was a great education from the other side. I learned a lot about the inner workings of a business that I was going to be in for 48 years."[18]

[17] Louie Robinson, "Quincy Jones: Man Behind the Music," *Ebony*, June 1, 1972
[18] Academy of Achievement

TRAIT #7 - I create

Jones received his first Grammy Award in 1963, for his arrangement of Count Basie's "I Can't Stop Loving You." (He went on to become the most nominated Grammy artist of all time with 79 nominations, winning 27 over the course of his career.) (TRAIT #7)

Four years earlier, Jones had arranged a benefit concert for Frank Sinatra in Monte Carlo. After it was over, Jones recalls, "All he said was, 'Cuckoo. Good job, kid.' That was it. Four years went by, and you don't know whether you connected. You can't call him and say, 'I want to work with you, Mr. Sinatra.' It don't work like that." But soon after the Count Basie recording came out, Jones got a call from Kauai. It was Frank Sinatra.

"'Hey Q, this is Francis.' We called him Francis, and he was the first person that ever called me Q," Jones explains. "'I just heard the album you did with Basie, and what you did to Bart Howard's song.'" (The song, "In Other Words," aka "Fly Me to the Moon," was originally a waltz, and Jones arranged it for Count Basie as a swing instrumental.) "'That's the way I want to do it,' he said. 'Would you consider doing an album with me and Basie?' Man, I said, 'Is the Pope a Catholic? Are you kidding?' Two days later I was over there in Hawaii. I worked with Frank from '64 until he died."

When he began working with Sinatra, he points out that he was ready. "Four trumpets, four trombones, five saxes, and four rhythm, strings, woodwinds and percussion. Symphony orchestra. Just like I did with Nadia Boulanger, you know."

He and Sinatra became so close, when Quincy Jones' son, Quincy III, was born, the infant received a letter from him. "'Dear Q3,'" Jones says, reciting the letter from memory. "'Let Uncle Frank welcome you to the world with a college education.' He had a bond in there to pay for his whole college education, knowing it would be a far better world than the one we screwed up. He was a real man. No bullshit. Never had a contract with him, it's a handshake, man. Never, ever, ever thought about my pal, because he always took care of me."

Jones goes on to credit Sinatra with ending racism in Las Vegas. "Because Lena Horne, and Belafonte, and all those guys, used to eat in the kitchen. They couldn't go in the casinos, and had to stay across town. It was sick. In 1964. Crazy, man. Frank didn't play, you know. Between Sammy, Basie, and myself, he ended it."

Sinatra's cover of "Fly Me to the Moon," with Q's arrangement, was the first recording ever played on the moon—Buzz Aldrin played it after touching down on the lunar surface. Some years later, Jones recalls, "We had a celebration at the space museum, with Neal Armstrong, John Glenn, and Buzz Aldrin. It was just amazing. And Frank was like a little kid. It was great."

Jones had wanted to score movies since he was a boy, and he got his chance in 1963 when Sidney Lumet asked him to provide the score for *The Pawnbroker.* Then he met Sidney Poitier, already a successful film star.

"You know how many of my movies he did the music for?" Poitier asks, reminiscing about Jones. "A goodly part of such success as I might have had, came from him."

Jones demurs. "Sidney was kind enough to hand me one of the batons. I did five films with him."

Those five included *In the Heat of the Night, For Love of Ivy* and *They Call Me Mr. Tibbs.*

Q scored thirty-three major films, including *In Cold Blood, The Italian Job, Bob & Carol & Ted & Alice, The Out of Towners, The Color*

*Purple,* and many, many more, along with countless scores for TV movies and series.

"You let the eye go in one direction, the ear in the other," he explained to *Ebony,* "and you let the audience participate somewhere in between."[19]

In 1974, Jones had a near-death experience when an aneurysm burst in his brain. The doctors saved him—but then discovered a *second* aneurysm that was ready to rupture. It was repaired surgically, but his doctors weren't sure he was going to survive.

It changed the way he looked at life and relationships. "I no longer take a lot of the crap off people that I used to take," he told *Ebony.* "I realize that time is too short to play games with anybody, and that they have to come to me straight. Everything has seemed so much clearer since my operation."[20]

In 1978, he received an Emmy for his score for the first episode of the groundbreaking TV miniseries *Roots.*

Throughout most of the 1980s, he produced albums for Michael Jackson, including *Bad* and *Thriller.* "A lot of the jazz musicians, when I did Michael Jackson, they said, 'You sold out.' I said, 'What do you mean sold out? I've been doing this all my life.' It's not even a stretch, you know, to go from different kinds of music."[21] (TRAIT #11) He remembers what he learned from Nadia Boulanger: "She would say, 'Quincy, there's only twelve notes until God gives us thirteen.' So

---

[19] Robinson
[20] Charles L. Sanders, "Ebony Interview with Quincy Jones," Ebony, October 1985
[21] Academy of Achievement

---

TRAIT #11 - I challenge the status quo

nothing scares me. Nothing scares me. From the symphony orchestra down, rhythm and blues, bebop, hip hop, salsa."

Also in the 1980s he launched his own record label, Qwest. The artists who recorded for him included Sarah Vaughn, Sinatra, and the punk band, New Order.

"And you look back later on and you say, 'How the hell did it happen?'"

In 1985 he produced the charity single, *We Are The World,* which raised money to help feed famine victims in Africa. At the time, he spoke about how his brush with death gave him the strength to take on the pressure and responsibility, which otherwise would have terrified him. *We Are the World* became the number one single of all time, raising over $60 million for famine relief.

At the same time, he became the Executive Producer of the film, *The Color Purple.* He had been looking for the right movie to produce for years, when he stumbled across Alice Walker's novel. "As soon as I read *The Color Purple,* I knew it was what I'd been looking for," he told *Ebony.*[22]

Now he just had to get the director he wanted: Steven Spielberg.

"When we started *The Color Purple,* the head of every studio said what's the matter with this idiot? He's got his first picture and he thinks he's gonna get Steven Speilberg? Steven was the biggest director in the history of film." But the studio heads didn't know that the two had already met, while Q was doing "Thriller" and Spielberg was shooting E.T. "He gave me a chair and a viewfinder, I gave him a synthesizer. We respected each other."

---

[22] Charles L. Sanders, "Ebony Interview with Quincy Jones," Ebony, October 1985

*The Color Purple*, directed by Spielberg and starring Whoopi Goldberg, Oprah Winfrey, and Danny Glover, was a box office blockbuster and received eleven Academy Award nominations.

Jones' 1989 album, *Back on the Block,* received the Grammy for Best Album of the Year, and included jazz heavyweights like Dizzy Gillespie, Miles David and Ella Fitzgerald along with contemporary stars like Ice T and Big Daddy Kane for the first fusion of be bop and hip hop.

In 1990 Jones founded *Vibe* magazine, and in 1991 he expanded to multimedia with the formation of Qwest Broadcasting. From 1990 to 1996, Jones Executive Produced the television series, *The Fresh Prince of Bel Air,* starring a very young Will Smith.

Jones attributes his success to maintaining an open mind. "I never turn my curiosity off," he says.[23] "My biggest problem in the world is going into a bookstore because everything—every subject from psychology to history to cuisine—everything in there, I'm interested in. (TRAIT #2) I love technology, biographies, history. Somehow all of those things reinforce each other."[24]

And he has a few words of advice for those hoping to make it in the world of music. (TRAIT #5) "Take a cram course in the business side of the entertainment business. You're crazy if you think that music is all you have to know."[25]

And don't give up, he says. "You don't learn a damn thing until you take a lot of chances and make a lot of mistakes. Love the mistakes.

---

[23] Sandy Cohen, "Quincy Jones: Kids, not career, are proudest achievement" AP (via KPIC. com), April 24, 2010, http://www.kpic.com/news/entertainment/92015409.html

[24] Academy of Achievement

[25] Charles L. Sanders, "Ebony Interview with Quincy Jones," Ebony, October 1985

---

TRAIT #2 - I am insatiably curious; TRAIT #5 - I delight in sharing what I do;
TRAIT #6 - I have the courage to take risks

All you gotta do to get my attention is say this is impossible, nobody's ever done this before." He continues, "You can't get an A if you're afraid of getting an F. Take chances. (TRAIT #6) Be inquisitive. Be nosey. And understand the bottom line is have humility with your creativity, and grace with your success."

Jones has never shied away from getting involved in causes he believes in. As he told *Ebony,* "You're divided between a concern for something that's bigger than any one person and having to make a living....But if you care about all of these things equally, you can't turn your mind off." [26] For instance, "I've been involved with South Africa and Nelson Mandela for 30 years. It's a way to really do something."[27] (TRAIT #12)

In 2001, Jones wrote *Q: The Autobiography of Quincy Jones,* which hit the NY Times, LA Times and Wall Street Journal's bestseller lists, adding bestselling author to his list of achievements.

And Jones is still directly influencing the future of jazz, with the "Quincy Jones Global Gumbo Project," which he brought to the 2012 Montreux Jazz Festival. The line-up included young musicians, talented teens and twenty-somethings from around the world—North America, Azerbaijan, Cuba, Slovakia, and more.

"This is the best talent all over the planet," he told Reuters. "They blow my mind, they're so young," he said.[28]

---

[26] Robinson
[27] Academy of Achievement
[28] Stephanie Nebehay, "Quincy Jones brings jazz prodigies to Montreux stage", Reuters, July 2, 2012, http://in.reuters.com/article/2012/07/02/entertainment-us-montreux-quincy-idINBRE8610XX20120702

---

TRAIT # 12 - I shape the future

At the same time he co-produced an Arabic charity single, "Tomorrow/Bokra." The Arabic vocals were performed by twenty-four tops artists from sixteen countries in the Middle East and North Africa. The video for the catchy tune intercuts images of Jones leading the musicians in the studio with views of modern Middle Eastern cities and images of laughing, smiling children, playing ball and running joyfully through the streets. The single and the later album that grew out of it, shot to number one across the Middle East, and all proceeds go to organizations like the United Nations World Food Program and to fund education in music, arts and the humanities.

Says Jones, "My soul sings with pride that the people of the Middle East and North Africa have embraced the ideals of peace, hope and unity expressed in 'Bokra'."

"He's a music master, a genius," says Sidney Poitier, describing why Jones fits his definition of a Renaissance Man. "I think it's the degree to which the individual spends his life reaching, and what he reaches for—and we don't know what a man reaches for. He knows. He senses it within himself. And when he finds that, it feeds him. If he's a musician, if he's a writer, if he's an actor, he nurtures that inside.... It presents itself at times when he needs to be in touch with himself. And infinitely more with Q."

"I always made my dreams bigger than what I could accomplish," says Jones, "so I never could get satisfied."

If Jones has one addiction, it's traveling. "We just played Poland and Sweden last month. We're deeply involved with Asia now, Korea, China. We're doing a film in Brazil next year in IMAX. I've been traveling for sixty-five years, traveling everywhere on the planet, and

I love it. It just fascinates me so much. You've got to go to know it. If you don't go, you don't know. I've been everywhere on the planet, and I feel at home everywhere."

And Jones wonders what the future will bring. "We're going through a technological revolution that will be changing civilization, from a communications standpoint. The way people will receive information, through PCs, through fiber optics, through all the converging technologies—it's going to be quite sensational." But, he points out, "We still have to remember, everything starts with two things, a song or a story. That drives everything. That's the people with the blank page, no matter what platform it's put on. That's where we have to start." [29]

---

[29] Academy of Achievement

# Yvon Chouinard

---

**"Cause no unnecessary harm."**

*Rock climber, mountain climber, surfer, kayaker; founder and CEO of Chouinard Equipment, Ltd., and Patagonia; writer; environmentalist.* (TRAIT #1)

Most environmental damage is caused unintentionally, by people not questioning what they do, says Yvon Chouinard. When he set up an environmental assessment program to ask questions about what his own clothing company, Patagonia, was doing, their first question was, "Of all fibers used in making clothing, which are the most damaging and which are the least damaging?" (TRAIT #2)

Chouinard and his team thought it would be the synthetics, which are, after all, made of petroleum. But to their surprise they found

---

TRAIT #1 - I am outstanding in my field and exceptional in many areas;
TRAIT #2 - I am insatiably curious

out the most damaging fiber by far is 100% pure cotton, which uses petroleum, fertilizer, and 25% of the world's pesticides even though it occupies only 3% of the world's farmland.

"I took a trip to the San Juaquin Valley," he recalls, "and went to some cotton fields. Boy, that was an education. They're killing fields. There's nothing out there that's alive. There's no birds, there's no insects, there's no weeds. There's just these little canals of toxic water. The cancer rate's ten times normal, crop dusters flying right over the workers. There's no outlet, no river that goes to the ocean, so all of that flows out into low areas and creates these huge ponds. They hire these guys to sit on lawn chairs with shotguns to keep the water fowl from landing, so that they don't have chicks with three beaks and four legs and stuff like that.

"So I came back and said, okay, I don't want to be in business if I have to use industrially grown cotton. Cotton was 20% of our sales, and I said I don't care. I'm not going to do this."

Chouinard gave his company two years to get out of making anything out of industrially grown cotton. He was absolutely committed to switch to organically grown cotton, and he told his company, "Either we make this work, or we're never going to use cotton again." [1]

"No young kid growing up ever dreams of someday becoming a businessman," Yvon Chouinard told a rapt lecture hall at UC Santa

---

[1] Voices - A UCSB Series, "The Education of a Reluctant Businessman with Yvon Chouinard" Presented by Arts & Lectures UC Santa Barbara, 2008, https://www.youtube.com/watch?v=NVfy2T0rzMc

Barbara in 2005. "Kids want to be firemen or forest rangers," he explained, "while businessmen are only heroes to other businessmen." Then, seeming to marvel at the odd journey his own life has taken, he said with a smile, "I wanted to be a fur trapper when I grew up"[2]

Chouinard still rejects the label "executive." (His refusal to use the word caused quite a stir some years back when he wrote "Capitalist" as his job description on a government form in China.[3]) His reticence may be due in part to the way he accidentally stumbled into being an entrepreneur through his love for the outdoors.

Born in a small French-Canadian town in Maine, his family moved to Southern California when Yvon was seven and they ended up in Burbank. Although he spoke no English he was put in elementary school—which, he says, lasted about three days. "I spent my early childhood in the hills above Griffith Park, and high school days hopping freights around the country. Spent a lot of days in jails,"[4] he told the UCSB audience with a laugh (and to some applause).

Starting a business must have been the furthest thing from his mind when, at twelve years old, Yvon found a passion, falconry.

As he recalls, a group of adults were willing to put up with some enthusiastic little kids and teach them love for the sport. "Falconry taught me a lot of things[5]," Chouinard told an audience at a symposium held at UCLA in 2011. "After you trap a wild bird, the first thing you do is you put him on your fist with these jesses" (thin leather straps

---

[2] Voices - UCSB
[3] Patt Morrison, "Yvon Chouinard: Capitalist Cat", Los Angeles Times, March 12, 2011, http://articles.latimes.com/2011/mar/12/opinion/la-oe-morrison-chouinard-031111
[4] Voices - UCSB
[5] UCLA Institute of the Environment, The Oppenheim Lecture Series, "Reflections of a Green Business Pioneer with Yvon Chouinard" https://www.youtube.com/watch?v=AoXkUmmAetM&feature=relmfu

that falconers use to tether their birds). "Then he flies off and you put him back on, he flies off, and you put him back on. You keep doing that until finally he sits there. And you stay up all night, until at last he falls asleep on your hand early in the morning. That's a real quick way to build trust in the bird." He pauses, then points out, "That was kind of my first lesson in Zen, because a Zen master would say, just who's getting trained here?"[6]

To check on the falcons in their nests—aeries built into crevices high in rocky crags—he learned to rappel down the cliffs. He soon fell in love with the art of rock climbing as an activity in itself.

Chouinard and his friends started hopping the train to Stoney Point in Chatsworth, a three hundred foot tall sandstone cliff jutting out of the ground near the northern end of Topanga Canyon Boulevard. At the age of sixteen he climbed his first mountain in Wyoming, and was hooked. (TRAIT #9)

At the time, most mountain climbers used pitons made of soft iron. The spikes were hammered into cracks in the rock and the climbers used them and ropes to support their weight as they climbed. European climbers traditionally left their pitons in place for the next group of climbers. This attitude didn't sit well with Chouinard: "We were brought up reading John Muir, and Thoreau, and Emerson, and we had an attitude that you go into the mountains and don't leave any trace of having been there."[7]

So when he was eighteen, Chouinard bought a used forge and an anvil along with some hammers and a book on blacksmithing,

---

[6] UCLA Institute of the Environment
[7] Voices - UCSB

TRAIT #9 - I am passionate

and taught himself to blacksmith. He started making pitons out of hard steel, which he could hammer in and then pull back out and use again.

These pitons became quite popular with Chouinard's friends and other climbers. He could forge two an hour and he began selling them out of his car for $1.50 each. It wasn't a lot of money, but it was enough to support himself as he drove from Big Sur to San Diego, breaking up his blacksmithing with rock climbing and surfing. Business was good, he added a few more items, and his improved pitons led to the rising popularity of rock climbing.

Chouinard and his friends, challenging themselves further, went to Yosemite, Canada, the Alps, and made spectacular climbs, becoming known, pushing the edge. Simultaneously, demand for his gear was increasing. In 1965, if a serious climber was doing a ten day climb up a rock wall in Yosemite, he had to have Chouinard's pitons. It would be impossible to carry 300 of the old-style ones, they would be too heavy. But a climber could carry thirty of Chouinard's, reusing each one ten times on the way up.[8] He went into business with his friend, Tom Frost, a climber and aeronautical engineer, and they founded Chouinard Equipment, Ltd.

In the late 1960s, Chouinard introduced improved crampons and ice axes, the tools of ice climbing, making it possible to scale steeper ice, turning ice climbing into a modern sport. "Every time I looked at a piece of equipment, I had an idea on how to make it better," Chouinard recalled. "Over the course of years, we basically redesigned

---

[8] UCLA Institute of the Environment

TRAIT #7 - I create

every single piece of climbing equipment."[9] (TRAIT #7) By 1970, the company was the largest supplier of climbing gear in the United States, and Chouinard's chrome-molybdenum steel pitons accounted for 70% of their business.

But Chouinard realized there was a problem: his pitons were causing serious damage to the rock walls. He saw it for himself during an ascent he made on El Capitan in Yosemite—where the popular route had formerly been unblemished, it was now deeply scarred and pitted.

Some years earlier, Upton Sinclair had written, "It is difficult to get a man to understand something when his salary depends upon his not understanding it." Yvon Chouinard was an anomaly to this rule. Even though the majority of his income came from the manufacture and sale of his pitons, he understood at once it was not worth the widespread damage they were causing. That damage was forever.

He and his partners immediately stopped selling the pitons and developed an alternative, environmentally-friendly way to climb. (TRAIT #6) "We came up with some ideas for these little aluminum chocks," small wedge-shaped pieces of aluminum threaded with wire, "that you just place with your fingers and you take out with your fingers and it doesn't damage the rock."[10] These chocks appeared in Chouinard's 1972 catalogue, along with a powerful essay extolling the virtues of "clean climbing:" leaving no trace of the climber's ascent, so later climbers would encounter the rock walls in their natural state.

---

[9] UCLA Institute of the Environment
[10] UCLA Institute of the Environment

---

TRAIT #6 - I have the courage to take risks

Confounding predictions of his company's demise, Chouinard revolutionized rock climbing. As piton use virtually ended, his business thrived, and the new chocks were ordered faster than they could be produced.

A few years earlier, during a climbing trip to Scotland, Chouinard had purchased a rugby shirt. "I thought it would make a great climbing shirt, because it was a really tough material, it had a collar so the gear slings wouldn't cut into your neck, and it was real colorful—blue and yellow and red."[11] In those early days of climbing, sportswear for men was mostly monochromatic tans and grays and black. When Chouinard started climbing in his colorful rugby shirt, all of his friends wanted to know where he got it. He imported some, added them to his catalogue, and they sold out almost immediately. He started selling shorts and jackets, and soon his clothing line was taking on a life of its own.

Chouinard and his business partners realized they needed to create a new identity for their clothing separate from the existing climbing equipment, and in 1972 *Patagonia* was born. They chose the name because "to most people, especially then, Patagonia was a name like Timbuktu or Shangri-La, far-off, interesting, not quite on the map." To their minds, it summoned up "romantic visions of glaciers tumbling into fjords, jagged windswept peaks, gauchos and condors."[12] (TRAIT #4)

The business boomed, sales grew year over year, they opened retail stores and in 1990 expected their sales to increase fifty percent—but instead a recession hit and they almost lost the business. Chouinard had

---

[11] Voices - UCSB

[12] Patagonia: Our History, http://www.patagonia.com/us/patagonia.go?assetid=3351

TRAIT #4 - I merge my left brain and my right brain

to lay off a fifth of his workforce, including many friends, the hardest thing he ever had to do, and he realized "my company had become part of the problem. We were completely unsustainable."[13]

They saved the company, but Chouinard saw his business needed to be completely reimagined. "Another Zen lesson that I learned is that you do a ten day climb on El Capitan [in Yosemite] and you get to the top and guess what? There's nothing there. It's just flat up there. So what's important is how you climb."[14] It's a lesson he applied to business. "You don't focus on making a profit. You focus on the process, and the profits will happen. It's the same thing with climbing, if you focus too much on getting to the summit, you'll blow it. You'll compromise on the way up."[15] (TRAIT #10)

He took the top ten people in the company to the real Patagonia in Argentina, and asked them all to consider why they were in business. None of them had ever planned to be businessmen, none of them had business degrees. What did they hope to accomplish?

Together, they made a statement of their core values:

• *Make the best quality products for their customers*. As a company that started out by making life-saving equipment for climbers, this was a no-brainer. None of them were willing to compromise on that. It did, however, open up a fruitful discussion on the definition of "quality."

• *Blur the distinction between work, play and family*. Mothers were encouraged to bring their babies into work, and Patagonia started one of the first corporate on-site child care centers in America.

---

[13] Voices - UCSB
[14] Voices - UCSB
[15] UCLA Institute of the Environment

---

TRAIT #10 - I have vision

• *Hire people with passion.* They all agreed they'd prefer to hire passionate outdoor people and train them in business, rather than hire businesspeople and try to convince them to love the outdoors.

• *Mandate time off for expeditions and surfing.* "We have a company policy that when the surf comes up everyone who's a serious surfer drops their work and they go surfing."[16] As long as the work gets done, Chouinard doesn't care when they do it.

As Chouinard went about rebuilding his company from this more enlightened perspective, he began to consider the worldwide degradation of the natural environment. He knew he had to add another piece to his company's mission statement:

• *Cause no unnecessary harm.* He notes that the statement couldn't be cause *no* harm because "there's no way you can ever manufacture a product without causing harm." It's the second law of thermodynamics, he explains. "You probably end up with more waste than you end up with final product. There's no such thing as sustainability."[17]

But he knew they could do better than they were doing. "I think every company has a responsibility to not only know what goes into the product, but to do something about it once you find out that you're doing something wrong." [18]

The first step was to admit that they were polluters, using up non-renewable resources. With that in mind, Chouinard began examining every aspect of his company.

"We decided to put our company on a path to where we'd be here a hundred years from now." They limited growth, turning away

---

[16] Voices - UCSB
[17] Voices - UCSB
[18] "How to Simply Your Life," An interview with Yvon Chouinard presented by Seventh Generation, 2010 https://www.youtube.com/watch?v=O3TwULu-WJw&feature=related

TRAIT #5 - I delight in sharing what I do

business when they could. They took out an ad encouraging people to buy products only when they actually needed them, not simply when they wanted them. (TRAIT #5)

"For me," Chouinard says, "the most enjoyable part of business, since I'm kind of a contrarian, is breaking the rules and then making it work. (TRAIT #11) If we grow three percent, four percent a year, we can be very profitable at that."[19]

Chouinard began the process of determining the environmental impact of his company which led to his discovery of the harm caused by the industrial farming of cotton. When he mobilized his company to switch to organic cotton without sacrificing quality, it was far more difficult than he had imagined. Occasionally, he says, he had to co-sign on loans because the banks wouldn't give farmers money to grow organic cotton; he had to find a cotton gin that would process the organic fiber. They found a company in Germany that produced non-toxic dyes, and one dye house in Portugal that didn't pollute the water. "It wasn't easy, but we did it. We convinced them that this was going to be the future, and we made it work."[20] (TRAIT #8)

In addition, they learned that their synthetic materials could also be produced more sustainably by using recycled materials. A fleece jacket, for instance, could be produced from twenty-five plastic quart-size soda bottles turned into polyester fiber.[21]

Chouinard next became concerned about what happens to his company's products after they've outlived their usefulness. Believing that his company is responsible for a product from its creation to its

---

[19] Voices - UCSB
[20] Voices - UCSB
[21] Yvon Chouinard & Vincent Stanley, *The Responsible Company*, Patagonia Books, 2012, p. 51

TRAIT #8 - I persevere; TRAIT #11 - I challenge the status quo

disposal and beyond, in 2005 Patagonia began a recycling program called Common Threads. Customers were told they could bring back worn out polyester products which would be recycled into new fiber and turned into new products. This had never been done before with clothing.

Chouinard wanted to increase the recycling program to include their entire line of products, but while polyester is fairly easy to recycle, cotton and other fibers are much more difficult. Customers were encouraged to follow the four R's: *reduce* (buy only what they need), *repair* (when necessary, before discarding), *reuse* (by donating or reselling the items they no longer use), and then finally *recycle*. By 2011, customers could bring any worn-out product they purchased from Patagonia back to the store to be recycled.[22]

Since 1986, Chouinard saw to it that Patagonia donated 10% of profits or 1% of sales (whichever was greater) to "the preservation and restoration of the natural environment."[23] They've donated over $45 million to domestic and international environmental groups and non-profits. In 2002, he co-created the "1% for the Planet" program to encourage other small companies and large corporations to do the same, and nearly 1,500 firms are now active participants in the program. (TRAIT # 12)

Chouinard's and Patagonia's concern about responsibility did not stop at the natural world, but also included the conditions of their workers. (TRAIT #3) In 1999, Patagonia joined a task force to end world-wide child labor and improve conditions for garment factory

---

[22] Chouinard & Stanley, p. 62-3
[23] Patagonia, "Environmentalism: What We Do", http://www.patagonia.com/us/patagonia. go?assetid=1960

TRAIT #3 - I embrace culture; TRAIT # 12 - I shape the future

workers. Since the early 2000s, Patagonia has taken care to examine every step of their supply chain, ensuring that a member of their team visits each factory on the chain before it comes on line, to make sure they are paying a decent wage and providing a healthy and well-lit workspace.[24]

As an author, Chouinard has described the life of an active outdoorsman in *Climbing Ice*, the experience of running a progressive company in *Let My People Go Surfing*, and the lessons he has learned from running Patagonia, *The Responsible Company*.

In *The Responsible Company*, Chouinard admits that, for all they've done, Patagonia is not yet a responsible company. They don't yet do everything they could do, and no manufacturing activity is completely sustainable. But as they continue to assess their impact on the environment and society, they are taking responsibility where they can, step by step.

Just like climbing a mountain, it's a process.

---

[24] Chouinard & Stanley, p. 58-59

# Elon Musk

---

**"If the economics of a technology are bad, then the technology is bad."**

*Businessman, scientist, physicist, designer, CEO of PayPal, Tesla Motors, SpaceX; Executive Producer of Thank You for Smoking; inspiration for the characterization of Iron Man; Goal: A multi-planetary future for humanity.* (TRAIT #1)

"When I was in college," Elon Musk told Wired Magazine during their first Google+ Hangout (a live video chat on Google's upstart social network), "I thought what are the things that are most going to affect the future of humanity? What are the most important problems that need to be solved, in my opinion, where one could apply technology to solve them.

"And the three things that I came up with were the internet, sustainable energy and space exploration—particularly making life multi-planetary."[1] (TRAIT #11)

---

[1] Adam Mann and Jason Paur, "Wired's Interview with SpaceX's Elon Musk," Wired Science, http://www.wired.com/wiredscience/2012/04/elon-musk-hangout/

TRAIT #1 - I am outstanding in my field and exceptional in many areas;
TRAIT #11 - I challenge the status quo

A multi-planetary future for humanity? Many college men dream of how they'd like to make the world a better place. The former head of PayPal (before eBay purchased it for $1.3 billion) and current head of both SpaceX and Tesla Motors, Musk seems well on his way to doing so. His comments came in April 2012, just a few days before his SpaceX Dragon spacecraft was due to dock with the International Space Station, a first for a private company.

"In terms of the internet, it's like humanity acquiring a collective nervous system," he says, and compares humanity before the internet to the hydra, a simple, multi-celled water creature which Musk describes as "a collection of cells that communicate by diffusion. With the advent of the internet, it was like we suddenly got a nervous system. In terms of the human collective, it's a hugely impactful thing."

Number two on his list, sustainable energy, "is the single biggest problem of the 21st century. We either solve that or we're screwed. It's tautological."

But he saves most of his passion for the goal of his life, which would literally change the world: a self-sustaining colony on Mars. (TRAIT #9) For "the last four billion years, life has been confined to earth— life as we know it, at least." He thinks it's time for a change. If some disaster befalls Earth, humanity will be extinguished, and consciousness could disappear from the universe. "I think we should apply some of our resources to prevent that from occurring."

For a self-sustaining colony to exist, he stresses the need for testing rockets. As he noted to Businessweek in a later interview, "I would like to die on Mars. Just not on impact."[2]

---

[2] Ashlee Vance, "Elon Musk, the 21st Century Industrialist," Bloomberg Businessweek/ Technology, Sept. 13, 2012, http://www.businessweek.com/articles/2012-09-13/elon-musk-the-21st-century-industrialist#p1

TRAIT #9 - I am passionate

*Esquire* named Elon Musk one of the 75 Most Influential People of the 21st century. *Forbes* called him one of America's 20 Most Powerful CEOs 40 and Under. *Time* put him on the Time 100, their 2010 list of the world's hundred most influential people. The brief accompanying profile, written by Jon Favreau, director of *Iron Man* and its sequels, acknowledged the young billionaire Musk as the inspiration for Robert Downey Jr.'s performance as Tony Stark.[3] He wrote: "Elon is a paragon of enthusiasm, good humor and curiosity—a Renaissance man in an era that needs them."[4]

Elon (his first name means "oak tree" in Hebrew) was born in Pretoria, South Africa, in 1971. Even early on, his curiosity was voracious. According to his mother, he read the entire Encyclopedia Britannica at the age of nine "and remembered it!"[5] (TRAIT #2)

By the time he was fifteen years old, Musk saw how limited his life in Pretoria would be, and he resolved to move to the United States. His mother's status as a Canadian citizen allowed him to move to that country. He spent a year or two couch-surfing with relatives and doing odd jobs. (The oddest, he commented in Businessweek: cleaning out boilers in a lumber mill, which involved shoveling "steaming goop" in a hazmat suit.[6])

Finally he was allowed admission to the United States to go to college. At the Wharton School, he studied economics and got his business degree, and the University of Pennsylvania awarded him a degree in physics. He took a job working on high energy density ultra-

---

[3] Jon Favreau, The 2010 Time 100: Thinkers: Elon Musk, http://www.time.com/time/specials/packages/article/0,28804,1984685_1984745_1985495,00.html

[4] Favreau

[5] Hannah Elliott, "The (Formerly) Fast Times Of the (Soon-to-Be) Bachelor (Multi) Billionaire," ForbesLife, April, 2012

[6] Vance

TRAIT #2 - I am insatiably curious

capacitors to assess their battery potential for electric vehicles,[7] then began a graduate program in science and business at Stanford.

But he left Stanford after two days when an opportunity from the world of business beckoned: on a shoestring, Musk co-founded Zip2 Corp in 1995, which provided online content to the New York Times and other newspapers.[8] (TRAIT #6) In 1999, Compaq paid over $300 million to buy the firm, and Musk found himself a millionaire by the age of twenty-eight.

Musk used some of these millions to co-found X.com, a new internet venture dedicated to making online purchases easier to complete. His company bought a little application called PayPal in 2000, which soon became the world's standard internet payment system. Musk was PayPal's Chairman and largest shareholder when eBay purchased the company in 2002.

Having helped find a way to monetize the Internet, Musk turned to his other passions. First up, the conquest of space.

In 2002, Musk founded SpaceX, short for Space Exploration Technologies, becoming its CEO and Chief Designer. He leased a shuttered aircraft assembly plant near LAX from Boeing, and turned the series of buildings into a rocket factory. The huge engine assembly floor gives way to the engineering section's rows and rows of cubicles and computer screens. For efficiency and perhaps to save time, Musk's own large desk has a conference table attached to it where he routinely meets with engineers and marketing people.

---

[7] Tesla Motors, About Tesla / Elon Musk,
http://www.teslamotors.com/about/executives/elonmusk
[8] Mary Bellis, About.com Inventors: Elon Musk;
http://inventors.about.com/od/mstartinventions/p/Elon-Musk.htm

---

TRAIT #6 - I have the courage to take risks

In 2008, SpaceX received a $1.6 billion contract from NASA to launch twelve cargo flights to the International Space Station. According to Businessweek, SpaceX will be able to transport astronauts to the space station for $20 million each, as opposed to the $63 million it costs NASA today.

Musk sees the financials as incredibly important, and one of his key advantages. "You cannot separate the economics from any given technology. If the economics of a technology are bad, then the technology is bad. That's all there is to it."[9]

At the same time as he was speaking to Wired Magazine's Google+ Hangout, the spacecraft that would carry out his company's first mission to dock with the space station was undergoing tests.

"We have an all-new docking system, it's never been tested before, that's going to go and acquire the space station, lock onto the space station, then plot an approach vector, and maneuver itself over to dock with the space station. It's a robotic spacecraft that's operating under its own intelligence. It pauses at various points and asks for authority to proceed, but it's really going under its own control for the vast majority of the flight."[10]

Questioned about the lack of a human astronaut on board the spacecraft, Musk points out, "I think it's a lot safer to have it be computer controlled. In the initial test phase I think it's great we're able to do it on an automated basis because we're not risking loss of life."[11]

He also pointed out that computers have always played a large part in space exploration. "Even in the days of Apollo, they still had

---

[9] Mann and Paur
[10] Mann and Paur
[11] Mann and Paur

quite a bit of computer assistance." Of course, he notes, computers were vastly more primitive then. "Your iPhone has more computing power than the entire Apollo program, which is kind of hard to imagine." Now that we have so much of that computing power available to us, "it makes sense to make use of it, and alleviate the need to have someone on board the spacecraft maneuvering it into position."

Musk also points out that once astronauts are on board, there *will* be a manual override. "So if something unexpected goes wrong, and it's not in the software to correct it, there will be a joystick, you will be able to control it when there are people on board."

When pressed on the point that fighter pilots onboard test flights added a dash of romance, Musk laughs, "I think software engineers are the fighter pilots of the new generation."[12]

On May 25, 2012, at 9:56 a.m. Eastern Time, the SpaceX Dragon successfully docked with the International Space Station, and began transferring needed supplies.[13]

SpaceX is now preparing for its first manned flights in 2015. As Musk explained to Stephen Colbert, during an appearance on his show, "We want to carry NASA astronauts and also carry private citizens to space, and long term we hope to be able to carry people beyond earth orbit. I really think that private enterprise is the future for space transportation, just as it is in air transport and road transport and ships."[14]

---

[12] Mann and Paur

[13] Matt Lynley, "Elon Musk Is The Most Inspiring Entrepreneur In The World", Business Insider, May 25, 2012,
http://www.businessinsider.com/congratulations-elon-musk-2012-5#ixzz2BNvzKGyO

[14] Colbert Report with Elon Musk, July 28, 2010,
http://www.colbertnation.com/the-colbert-report-videos/341483/july-28-2010/elon-musk

As he modestly described himself to Colbert, "I'm mostly an engineer, I design things."[15] At least it sounded modest, but as he later clarified to Bloomberg TV: "An engineer is the closest thing to a magician that exists in the real world."[16] (TRAIT #4)

In 2003, Musk turned his attention to his third goal, sustainable energy, by co-founding Tesla Motors. According to the company's website, Musk is Chairman, Product Architect and CEO.[17] (TRAIT #7)

The original Tesla Roadster, an all-electric, super-expensive, sports car, was designed to put Tesla Motors on the map. In 2012, they released the more affordable Model S, the world's first luxury electric sedan, and the even more affordable Model X, an SUV/minivan designed for active families. Musk owns 29% of Tesla, a company now valued at more than $3 billion.[18]

If Tesla remains an exclusive brand available only to elites, even if the company survives, Musk will perceive it as a failure. "Our target in the long term," Musk told Colbert, "is to make mass-market electric cars" that cost under $30,000.[19] (TRAIT #5)

In addition to developing their own cars, Musk has made strategic deals with car companies Daimler and Toyota worth millions of dollars, to sell them electric powertrain system. As he explained in an appearance on the Charlie Rose show: "Sometimes the media tries to create more of an antagonistic position than is really the case. I'm

---

[15] Colbert Report
[16] BloombergTV, Aug. 3, 2012,
http://www.bloomberg.com/video/73460184-elon-musk-profiled-bloomberg-risk-takers.html
[17] Tesla Motors
[18] Elliott
[19] Colbert Report

TRAIT #4 - I merge my left brain and my right brain; TRAIT #5 - I delight in sharing what I do; TRAIT #7 - I create

actually really supportive of any efforts like the Volt or the Leaf or anything that goes in the direction of sustainable transport."[20]

Musk now divides his week between SpaceX (Mondays and Thursdays), which is located in Hawthorne, just southeast of LAX, and Tesla Motors (Tuesdays and Wednesdays), headquartered in Palo Alto. (He spends Fridays at both SpaceX and a nearby satellite Tesla office devoted to design).

In 2006, Musk co-founded SolarCity. Demonstrating his seriousness about the need for alternative, renewable sources for energy to combat global warming and reduce air pollution, SolarCity designs, manufactures and installs solar panels on homes and businesses.

In July 2011, through the Musk Foundation, SolarCity donated a solar powered generating station to Soma, Japan, after the city was hit by an earthquake and tsunami in March of that year, and the Fukushima Daiichi nuclear power plant went offline. They also donated solar power to the hurricane response center in Alabama for victims of Hurricane Katrina and the Gulf oil spill. (TRAIT #12)

Musk began developing another transportation project in 2012, something he calls the Hyperloop. Although he won't disclose details, it's a tube system capable of moving a person from San Francisco to Los Angeles in thirty minutes. "What you want is something that never crashes, that's at least twice as fast as a plane, that's solar powered and that leaves right when you arrive, so there is no waiting for a specific departure time," he told the Business Insider.[21]

---

[20] The Charlie Rose Show with Elon Musk, Nov. 9 2011, http://www.charlierose.com/view/interview/11984
[21] Jay Yarow, "California is Going to Burn Money on a Bullet Train," Business Insider, Sept. 14, 2012, http://www.businessinsider.com/elon-musks-hyper-loop-2012-9#ixzz2DPjcqavV

TRAIT #12 - I shape the future

ForbesLife referred to Musk as an L.A. playboy, living in a 20,000 square foot mansion in Bel Air, with 1.6 acres in grounds, a tennis court and a view of the Pacific Ocean.[22] And Musk himself, on the Colbert show, acknowledged that he lives "large."[23]

That may be so, but few playboys own a coffee table engraved with the periodic table of elements.[24] And Musk remains voraciously curious: eBooks he's read recently include *The Autobiography of Benjamin Franklin* and *Steve Jobs* by Walter Isaacson,[25] and he calls Douglas Adams's *The Hitchhiker's Guide to the Galaxy* one of the most influential books he's ever read, because it taught him the difficult thing is to ask the right questions.[26] (TRAIT #3)

But Musk never forgets about his most serious goal: that of going to Mars. As he told Wired, "The reason I started SpaceX was because I think we needed to develop the technology necessary to make life multi-planetary, with Mars being the only realistic option for creating a base with a self-sustaining civilization. That's really what SpaceX has been about since I started it, to keep advancing the state of the art of rocket technology, and one of the metrics is how much does it cost to go to space. That's one of the most fundamental metrics. Of course, reliability is also important. And being able to create a rocket that's big enough to get to Mars is extremely important. So we've made steady progress in all those arenas. I'm increasingly confident that if

---

[22] Elliott
[23] Colbert Report
[24] Elliott
[25] Elliott
[26] Vance

---

TRAIT #3 - I embrace culture

we continue on this trajectory that we will develop the technology necessary to take people to Mars."[27] (TRAIT #8)

Musk isn't interested in what he refers to as a super-expensive "flags and footprints" mission to Mars, like the United States did with the moon. "That would set a new high altitude record and would be interesting," he acknowledges, but it wouldn't have a great impact on humanity. "I think what really matters is developing a system that's capable of transporting huge numbers of people and cargo to Mars, such that it can become a self-sustaining civilization." While the first trips will be round-trips, they need to eventually get "the cost of moving to Mars down to something that a middle-class person in American can afford. If we can do that, then I think it will occur, and will be a sort of a naturally self-sustaining reaction, and life will become multi-planetary." (TRAIT #10) This involves developing a new generation of rockets that can move thousands of people and tons of freight to Mars, and the economics will only work if the rockets can be brought back and reused. "I believe I have a design," he told Wired. "We're close."[28]

And then he brings it back to history and the settling of America. "That's really how the United States was formed. The cost of a trip to America got down to something that a relatively middle-class person in England could afford. So enough people chose to make that journey to form the beginnings of the United States."[29]

---

[27] Mann and Paur
[28] Mann and Paur
[29] Mann and Paur

---

TRAIT #8 - I persevere; TRAIT #10 - I have vision

# Steve Jobs

## (1955 - 2011)

**"Here's to the crazy ones."**

*Developed original Apple computer in his parents garage with friend Steve Wozniak; founder and CEO of Apple Computer; CEO of Pixar Studios, producer of TOY STORY, FINDING NEMO, etc.; ten years after being forced out, returned to Apple Computer and restored the company to profitability, introduced the iMac, iPod, iPhone and iPad, remaking Apple into a force in the tech sphere.* (TRAIT #1)

"It was much worse than I thought when I went back initially," Steve Jobs recalled in remarks at the eighth annual All Things Digital conference in 2010. He was talking about his return to Apple Computer in 1996, eleven years after he had been forced out of the company

---

TRAIT #1 - I am outstanding in my field and exceptional in many areas

he started. He discovered Apple was only about ninety days from bankruptcy. But he also found a secret weapon he could use to save the company: "I'd expected all the good people would have left. And I found these miraculous people, these great people" who had stayed through the changing regimes.

Jobs asked them, as tactfully as he could manage, "Why are you still here?" Most of them responded with a reference to Apple's original logo: "Because I bleed in six colors."

Jobs had to pause for a moment before he continued, "That was code for, 'because I love what this place stands for.' And that just made all of us want to work that much harder to have it survive."[1]

Such feelings reflect the passion of the man who started the company, the one who came back to save it.

Steve Job's return to Apple was just one in the series of journeys that comprised his life.

Even his birth was a journey, as his birth parents put him up for adoption days after he was born. He was adopted by a couple in Mountain View, California, just down the highway from Palo Alto, the future site of Silicon Valley.

Thanks to the words and attitude of his adoptive parents, he never felt abandoned. They told him he was *chosen.*

Steve was a reluctant, uninterested student who spent his time playing pranks. (A personal favorite: when he was in third grade, with a friend, he made posters for a made-up "Bring Your Pet to School Day." Many kids bought it, and dogs were chasing cats all over the school.[2])

[1] "Steve Jobs at the D8 Conference"
http://www.youtube.com/watch?v=LrS7JQv-zgY&feature=related
[2] Isaacson, *Steve Jobs*

A teacher saw his potential, and with his parents' support, the school realized how advanced he was and suggested skipping him ahead two years. He graduated at the top of his class where his classmates were the kids of scientists and engineers. (TRAIT #2)

One of the things that struck Jobs from the time he was young, was the power of asking for help. He never found anyone who wouldn't help him if he just asked. "I called up Bill Hewlitt when I was twelve years old," Jobs told the Santa Clara Valley Historical Assoc. Hewlitt, the founder of Hewlitt-Packard, was one of the titans of the early computer industry. "He lived in Palo Alto, his number was still in the phone book, and he answered the phone himself. I said, 'I'm Steve Jobs, I'm twelve years old, I'm a student in high school and I want to build a frequency counter, and I was wondering if you have any spare parts I could have.'

"And he laughed, and he gave me the spare parts to build this frequency counter, and he gave me a job that summer at Hewlitt Packard, on the assembly line putting nuts and bolts together on frequency counters. And I was in heaven. And I've never found anyone who said no or hung up the phone when I called. I just asked."

This is a very important point to Jobs. "Most people never pick up the phone and call, most people never ask. And that's what separates, sometimes, the people that do things from the people that just dream about them. You've got to act. And you've got to be willing to fail, you've got to be willing to crash and burn, with people on the phone, with starting a company, with whatever. If you're afraid of failing, you won't get very far."[3] (TRAIT #6)

---

[3] Steve Jobs Thoughts on Life, Santa Clara Valley Historical Association
http://www.youtube.com/watch?v=x8DdORZhBIM&feature=related

TRAIT #2 - I am insatiably curious; TRAIT #6 - I have the courage to take risks

Through a mutual friend, Steve Jobs met Steve Wozniak in 1969. Wozniak, five years older than Jobs, was working at HP designing what he termed the "hottest gadget" on the planet—the HP Scientific Calculators. (Within five years, Woz later would note, it changed the world, obliterating the slide-rule. Every engineer and scientist in the world had to have one.)

Once the two began working together, Wozniak could sense right away that Jobs was a leader who wanted to change the world. Whenever Woz came up with some new piece of technology, an item that he thought was simply "cute," Jobs wanted to sell it. This included a simple, handheld device he built that produced electronic telephone tones that allowed the user to dial anywhere in the world for free. Woz thought it would be fun to show off at parties, to be a comedian. "No," Woz recalled Jobs saying. "Let's sell it."

In 1974, a year and a half after dropping out of college, Jobs got a job at Atari. Due to his brashness and body odor (he believed his vegan diet would keep b.o. away), many of the engineers at Atari wanted to fire him. But the charismatic founder of Atari, Nolan Bushnell, liked the young man, and worked out a solution: they put him on the night shift.[4]

With the money he earned, Jobs left Atari and went to India, where he spent seven months, first trying to find a guru, then trying to find himself. Then he came back to Atari and asked for his job back, which he got.

Walter Isaacson, who wrote Steve Jobs' biography, interviewed Jobs more than forty times for the book. In a *60 Minutes* interview, Isaacson discussed the contradictions he saw in Jobs—he personified a

---

[4] Walter Isaacson, Steve Jobs, Simon & Schuster, 2011

mixture of the engineer culture and hippie counter-culture that existed then in San Francisco. He was a hippy-ish rebel who loved listening to Dylan and dropped acid, but he also loved electronics. These disparate impulses "came together in Steve Jobs."[5] (TRAIT #3)

In 1975, Jobs and Wozniak co-designed the game *Breakout* for Atari. Jobs convinced Woz that he could do it in four days. They stayed up three nights in a row to get the job done.

In 1976, Jobs and Wozniak began working on the first Apple computer in Jobs's parents' garage. As proud as they were of it, it was basically just a motherboard. It had no case, screen or keyboard, and was aimed at hobbyists who would assemble the rest of the device themselves. They showed it off at the Home Brew Computer Club, where the owner of a computer store suggested he could sell them if they put it in a case and added a keyboard.

Wozniak and Jobs realized it was time to put together a team and incorporate. At a press conference some years later, a then shaggy-haired, mustachioed and goateed Steve Jobs was asked how Apple Computers got its name. He explained how, when his team was preparing a "Fictitious Business Name Statement," they came up with all sorts of possibilities that nobody liked ("Matrix Electronics" was one example). [6]

"We simply decided that we were going to call it Apple Computer," he declared, "unless someone suggested a better name by five o'clock that day" when the form was due. Certainly there were some specific

---

[5] Walter Isaacson, 60 Minutes interview
[6] Steve Jobs: How Apple got its name, http://www.youtube.com/watch?v=qzzOwRx3D1E&feature=fvwp

TRAIT #3 - I embrace culture

reasons for choosing the name: "Partially because I like apples a lot, and partially because Apple is ahead of Atari in the phone book."[7]

"But we reexamined it on a regular basis, and we found the juxtaposition seemed to epitomize what we were going after, which was simplicity, and yet very refined sophistication." In fact, the title of their first brochure was, "Simplicity is the ultimate sophistication."

"And that wasn't just a bullshit slogan," Jobs emphasized. "It actually was really what we've been striving for, and Apple seemed to symbolize that." He grinned at the assembled reporters. "So I think we're gonna stick with it."[8]

In 1977, Jobs and Wozniak got an investor, former Intel exec Mike Markkula, and they created the Apple II, the first personal computer intended for a mass market (TRAIT #7). They introduced the product at the West Coast Computer Faire in April of 1977, a conference of hobbyists and exhibitors at the San Francisco Civic Auditorium. (Along with Apple Computers, exhibitors included such little-known entities as Smoke Signal Broadcasting and Parasitic Engineering.)

"My recollection is we stole the show," Jobs noted. "A lot of dealers and distributors started lining up, and we were off and running."[9]

Jobs and Wozniak placed an order with a local factory to produce one thousand units—a huge risk for them at the time.

Wozniak sums up their early days with one word: Courage. "You don't know if you can do it, and you're afraid to fail, but I'll tell you

---

[7] How Apple got its name
[8] How Apple got its name
[9] The History of Apple Computer, http://www.youtube.com/watch?v=eB55Wjy44cM&feature=related posted by SilverBackStudios

TRAIT #7 - I create

that drives you to try harder and work harder than you've ever done in your life."[10]

The Apple II was a huge success, and one of the things Jobs was proudest of was how Apple made great technology very accessible for so many people. (TRAIT #5)

"I was worth over a million dollars when I was 23, and over ten million dollars when I was 24, and over one hundred million dollars when I was 25, and it wasn't that important because I never did it for the money."[11]

In December 1979, Jobs was invited to Xerox Parc for a visit. As he recalled in a documentary, "They showed me three things, but I was so blinded by the first one that I didn't even really see the other two." The thing that blinded him was a demo of the Graphical User Interface, or GUI. Little icons of pieces of paper represented documents which could be placed into icons of folders, with a cursor that could be moved around the screen with a mouse. "I thought it was the best thing I'd ever seen in my life."

Jobs pointed out it was flawed, incomplete, and they had done a bunch of things wrong. But "the germ of the idea was there, and they'd done it very well. And within ten minutes it was obvious to me that all computers would work like this some day."[12]

As a Xerox PARC researcher put it, Jobs understood what their technology could do after an hour of looking at the demo, far more so than the executives at Xerox who had had years of exposure to it.

---

[10] Steve Wozniak Speaks About Apple,
http://www.youtube.com/watch?v=l1xeJpXrhjI&feature=related
[11] PBS, "Triumph of the Nerds"
[12] "Triumph of the Nerds"

---

TRAIT #5 - I delight in sharing what I do

Jobs shook his head in wonder that Xerox had no clue about what they had. "Xerox could have owned the entire computer industry today. It could have been a company ten times its size. It could have been IBM. It could have been Microsoft." But it was Jobs who had that vision. In exchange for a deal on 100,000 shares in Apple, Xerox essentially gave Jobs and his team the inspiration that became the Macintosh GUI.

Jobs was determined to release an entirely new computer with a breathtakingly short development schedule, and he managed to convince his team they could do it. He was famous for wielding one of the most powerful weapons a CEO could ever have: the "Reality Distortion Field." According to people who worked for him, he was able to "convince anyone of practically anything," and the RDF seemed as good an explanation as any for that ability.

As described by Andy Hertzfeld, who went to work for Apple in 1981, the reality distortion field was "a confounding mélange of a charismatic rhetorical style, an indomitable will, and an eagerness to bend any fact to fit the purpose at hand."[13]

In 1984, Apple introduced the Macintosh computer, utilizing the best elements of the perfected GUI. "Picasso had a saying. 'Good artists copy. Great artists steal,'" noted Jobs. "We have always been shameless about stealing great ideas. And I think part of what made the Macintosh great was that the people working on it were musicians and poets and artists and zoologists and historians who also happened to be the best computer scientists in the world."[14] (TRAIT #4)

---

[13] Andy Hertzfeld, Mac Folklore,
http://folklore.org/StoryView.py?project=Macintosh&story=Reality_Distortion_Field.txt
[14] History of Apple Computer

---

TRAIT #4 - I merge my left brain and my right brain

Around that time, Jobs hired John Scully, the former CEO of Pepsi to be CEO of Apple. They built a huge inventory of Macs, but the demand didn't materialize, costing the company millions of dollars. In 1985, Jobs was stripped of all his responsibilities, and he resigned from the company.

"What can I say? I hired the wrong guy. And he destroyed everything I spent ten years working for."

Steve Jobs founded NeXT Inc., with the goal of engineering a quantum leap forward in computer hardware and software. Most experts agree that the operating system he eventually developed to run the machine was state of the art, and a NeXT computer was used to create the World Wide Web, but it was never a commercial success.

About a year after he founded NeXT, Jobs purchased a little computer division from George Lucas (creator of *Star Wars* and owner of the visual effects company, Industrial Light & Magic).

As Jobs explained his decision to Charlie Rose on his PBS interview series, "I heard about this incredible group of computer graphic specialists that George Lucas had assembled at LucasFilm, that he wanted to sell. So I went up there and saw what they were doing." And he was blown away by their work. "I'd spent a lot of time in computer graphics with the Macintosh, but this was way beyond anything I'd seen. I bought into that dream both spiritually, if you will, and financially, and we bought the computer division from George and incorporated it as Pixar."[15]

It took Pixar ten years to develop and produce their first fully-computer-animated feature film—but in February of 1995, *Toy Story* was released.

---

[15] Steve Jobs and John Lasseter interview on Charlie Rose,
http://www.youtube.com/watch?v=E29v8vF0u-8

The movie was an instant smash at the box office, but it hadn't come easy. "It took us a long time to build the technical foundation to do this stuff. We were pioneering every step of the way. Pixar invented all this stuff. But we don't view ourselves as a technology company. Our product is content. We're an entertainment company, and all this technology really is just in the service of the storytelling."[16]

But Jobs knew he couldn't take the credit himself. "You've got to have an extraordinary team," he said, "because you're trying to climb a mountain with a whole party of people, a lot of stuff to bring up the mountain, so one person can't do it."[17]

The week after the film was released, the company went public. Steve Jobs was suddenly worth $1.5 billion.

Meanwhile, NeXT's commercial difficulties were rocking that company. Some of their largest investors pulled out. Without telling Jobs what he was doing, the Chief Operating Officer tried to tempt Sun, their chief competitor, into buying the company. And NeXT had to fire 300 employees as it divested its hardware side and became purely a software company.

At the same time, Apple was having problems of its own. It was losing market share. No one wanted its hardware. The new operating system the firm had sunk millions into and spent a decade developing wasn't working. They needed to find a modern operating system and turn the company around—fast! They realized their only hope was to buy a compatible OS from an outside source.

In 1996, eleven years after he had been forced out of the company he had created, Apple decided to buy NeXT Inc. for over $400 million.

---

[16] Charlie Rose
[17] Charlie Rose

With it came the services of Steve Jobs as a "special advisor" to Gil Amelio, Apple's CEO.

By the following year, Amelio was ousted from Apple, and Jobs was named interim CEO.

One of the first things Jobs did was simplify Apple's product line. Instead of the huge number of different models they were producing, he drew a chart with four boxes and told them they would only make four computers: a laptop and a desktop for professionals, and a laptop and a desktop for home users.

In 1998, for the first time in years, Apple was profitable again, thanks to their professional line of Power Macs.

Then Jobs turned to the home user, and the iMac was born.

Instead of a beige box, the computer was housed in a bright, colorful translucent skin. It was designed by Jonathan Ive, a British designer who joined Apple in 1992. Jobs made him head of design in 1998. Ive spoke to candy makers and tried many different plastics to get exactly the right color and level of translucency.

The reason for that much care was simple, as Ive explained to the BBC. "A lot of people at that point in time were nervous around computers, around technology. So our clear goal was how to make the product accessible and not intimidating." [18]

Jobs had his hand in every element of the design. "I think Steve is a design champion by action, not by talking about design," said Ive. "He not only has a very clear sort of vision, and sense of the future, but has this sort of unnerving ability to describe the future in a way that's very inclusive, in a way that draws people from many

---

[18] Jonathan Ive speaking to Nicholas Glass, Arts Editor of the BBC

TRAIT #10 - I have vision

different disciplines in to share this sense of what this vision could be."[19] (TRAIT #10)

According to Water Isaacson, Jobs's biographer, part of what impacted his design sense was his attraction to Zen simplicity. "That simplicity is the ultimate sophistication."[20]

Jobs considered what made Apple different, not just from other computer firms, but any other consumer product. "Everyone says they want to make a great product or they want to make a great movie, or whatever they're doing, so there's no difference there. But there's a big difference in outcomes."[21]And one of the differences was a result of Jobs' willingness to take the time to get it right, no matter what the cost. "Sometimes you just have to look at yourself and go, you know, it's just not really great," he explained. "It's okay. It's good. But let's not fool ourselves and call it great. We're willing to throw something away because it's not great and try again, when all of the pressures of commerce are at your back saying no, you can't do that." (TRAIT #8)

In 2003, Jobs was first diagnosed with pancreatic cancer. At first he tried alternative therapies, but eventually had the tumor surgically removed. He remained healthy for a number of years, long enough to release several new versions of the iMac, to make his well-known commencement speech at Stanford, for Pixar's *Finding Nemo* to win the Academy Award for Best Animated Feature, for the Walt Disney Company to acquire Pixar for over $7 billion, and to introduce the iPhone, which would radically transform Apple.

---

[19] "Steve Jobs on Design", http://www.youtube.com/watch?v=sPfJQmpg5zk&feature=endscreen
[20] Walter Isaacson, 60 Minutes interview
[21] "Steve Jobs on Design"

---

TRAIT #8 - I persevere

At the D5 conference in 2007, Jobs pointed out, "You have to have a lot of passion for what you're doing, because it's so hard that if you don't, any rational person would give up. And you have to do it over a sustained period of time. So if you don't love it, if you're not having fun doing it, you're going to give up. (TRAIT #9) And that's what happens to most people actually. If you really look at the ones that ended up being successful in the eyes of society and the ones that didn't, oftentimes the ones that are successful loved what they did so they could persevere when it got really tough. And the ones that didn't love it quit, because they're sane. Who would want to put up with this stuff if you didn't love it? So it's a lot of hard work, and it's a lot of worrying, constantly, and if you don't love it, you're gonna fail. So you gotta love it. And you gotta have passion." [22]

Reporter Walt Mossberg, one of the organizers of *AllThingsDigital* conferences, summed Jobs up this way: "He did what a CEO should: Hired and inspired great people; managed for the long term, not the quarter or the short-term stock price; made big bets and took big risks. He insisted on the highest product quality and on building things to delight and empower actual users, not intermediaries like corporate IT directors or wireless carriers. And he could sell. Man, he could sell."[23]

"The time we grew up in was a magical time," Jobs told Walter Isaacson during one of their interviews. "It was also a very spiritual time in my life."[24]

---

[22] Steve Jobs explains the rules for success,
http://www.youtube.com/watch?v=KuNQgln6TL0&feature=endscreen
[23] Walt Mossberg, "The Steve Jobs I Knew",
http://allthingsd.com/20121005/the-steve-jobs-i-knew/
[24] Isaacson, 60 Minutes

---

TRAIT #9 - I am passionate

Ironically, Isaacson pointed out on *60 Minutes*, when Jobs came back from his experience in India, he decided to become a businessman, building a primitive computer for hobbyists. Jobs had this tension within him between being hippyish and anti-materialistic, and wanting to create a business to sell things like Wozniak's board. He somehow melded the two sides of himself in an act of creation.

"In the end," as Issacson put it, "he wouldn't take no for an answer, and he would make the sort of dent in the universe he wanted to. He would bend reality and they would accomplish it."[25] (TRAIT #12)

Jobs laid his soul bare in the first ad he was responsible for when he came back to Apple Computer. Although he didn't write the copy himself, it was as personal a statement as ever appeared in a commercial for a billion dollar company. "Here's to the crazy ones...the misfits...the rebels...the troublemakers... (these words spoken over photos and film of Albert Einstein, Bob Dylan, Martin Luther King, and others) ...they push the human race forward...and while some may see them as the crazy ones...we see genius...because the people who are crazy enough to think they can change the world...are the ones who do." (TRAIT #11)

It ended with the words: Think different.

As Isaacson pointed out, this wasn't an ad, "but a manifesto."[26]

---

[25] Isaacson, 60 Minutes
[26] Isaacson, 60 Minutes

---

TRAIT #11 - I challenge the status quo; TRAIT #12 - I shape the future

# Steve Allen

## (1921 - 2000)

**"I have a philosophical concern that the
American public is getting dumber"**

*Television innovator (first host and co-creator of The Tonight Show),
comedian, actor, musician, composer (of 8,500 songs), author,
created the TV series, Meeting of the Minds.* (TRAIT #1)

Doris Day was not going to show, that much was certain. The
year was 1948. Perhaps it was a miscommunication between her and
her publicist, perhaps (as she later explained) she'd never been told she
was set to appear on the most popular radio show in Los Angeles.

Whatever the case, she had been scheduled and announced and
didn't show up, and now, at the last minute, Steve Allen, host of the

---

TRAIT #1 - I am outstanding in my field and exceptional in many areas

KNX radio comedy and interview show, found himself with half an hour of empty airtime to fill.

"There I was on the air live," Allen recalled, years later, to the Archive of American Television. "I'd already played my piano numbers and done my two or three pages of written comedy stuff, and I couldn't think of anything to do." So he grabbed the heavy floor microphone and carried it down to the studio audience and started interviewing the people who were there simply to watch him do his live radio show. "And the most remarkable thing happened," Allen marveled. "I'd been getting good laughs before, but I got laughs like I never got before as a comic, totally adlibbing. I don't know whether it was the desperation of the moment, or what, but I realized after the show, 'Hey, I've discovered something here.'"[1] In fact, he'd invented a bit—the live, impromptu, studio audience interaction—that has become a staple of every late-night TV talk show.

Stephen Valentine Patrick William Allen was born in Harlem, New York, on December 26, 1921. His parents were a popular vaudeville comedy team, known by the stage names Billy Allen and Belle Montrose. His father died when Steve was only eighteen months old, and when his mother went back on the road as a solo act, the toddler accompanied her some of the time. (The then-teenaged Milton Berle, who shared the bill with Steve's mom, babysat the toddler on more than a few occasions.) But vaudeville was no way to raise a child, so Steve was handed off to his mother's relatives, and he spent most of his youth in Chicago, being passed from one member of her family to another. He later credited the rapid-fire banter between his mother's family as helping him to develop his comedy chops.

---

[1] Archive of American Television, Interview with Steve Allen, http://www.emmytvlegends. org/interviews/people/steve-allen#

Allen got his first radio job in 1942, at KOY in Phoenix, where he produced his own comedy and music show. He enlisted in the army during World War II and trained for the infantry, but he was discharged because of his asthma before he ever served overseas.

In 1945, he created a five-night-a-week radio comedy show, *Smile Time*, for the Mutual Broadcasting System. (TRAIT #7) He later moved to CBS and their flagship Los Angeles radio station, KNX, where he was hired as a late-night DJ. L.A. was the largest radio market in the west, but just being a DJ felt like a step backwards to Allen, so he began spending more time talking and telling jokes than spinning records, and his show started to get more listeners.

Management balked, and ordered him to do what they had hired him to do—play records. Instead, Allen did something he later thought was either very dumb or very brave: he read their memo to him on the air, and asked the fans what they thought he should do. (TRAIT #6) Letters came in by the sack-full, supporting him and the direction his show was taking. Management backed off and Allen's popularity soared. (TRAIT #11)

Listeners began coming to the station to watch the show, so he was moved to Studio A, where Jack Benny and other big stars of the Golden Age of radio performed in front of large studio audiences. Allen's show was expanded to an hour—which he took as a compliment, but there was no corresponding increase in pay, so he wasn't inclined to spend more time in the office writing jokes. That's when inspiration struck.

"I'll interview people," he thought, and essentially invented the radio talk show. (TRAIT #10) He had on the big stars of his day, such as

---

TRAIT #6 - I have the courage to take risks; TRAIT #7 - I create; TRAIT #10 - I have vision; TRAIT #11 - I challenge the status quo

Rudy Vallee, Al Jolson, and Gloria Swanson, plugging their new movies, books and albums. And when Doris Day was a no-show that night, thanks to Allen's inspired response, he became even more popular, and was soon given a national audience through the CBS radio network. For the first time, his show had a budget and other writers. Known for pranks, Allen called for everyone listening to his show in a car to honk their horns simultaneously. Tens of thousands of cars across the country honked in unison.

In 1950, CBS moved Allen to TV as the morning host of the eponymously-named *The Steve Allen Show*. The show did not fare well, so CBS moved it to evening, and then cancelled it.

Allen was back on the bottom, but he didn't give up. (TRAIT #8) In 1953 he got a job as the host of a local, late night talk-variety show an NBC affiliate. It wasn't a large audience, but he got the thing he wanted most: creative control, and ad-libbing Q & A's with his studio audience was a mainstay. (When a woman asked if they got the show in Rochester, Allen quipped, "They see this show in Rochester. I don't think they get it.")

And the next year, his little local show went national as *The Tonight Show*. It was part interview show, somewhat like the *Tonight Show* of today, but "variety" was the key word: "For the first three years it was not a talk show every night but an experimental laboratory," he told *People* magazine in 1977. "I had almost total freedom to do any damn thing I wanted to do. One night we might book the Basie band, another night a debate about the blacklist, followed by a guest

---

TRAIT #3 - I embrace culture; TRAIT #8 - I persevere

appearance of the Harlem Globetrotters."[2] (TRAIT #3) Steve Allen was one of the first to air African-American performers on network television; he also introduced jazz to a national TV audience.

He left the show after only three years when NBC created a Sunday night show for Allen, to try to take down the reigning CBS champ: Ed Sullivan. Even though his show offered stars and musical acts from Elvis Presley and Fats Domino to Errol Flynn and Abbot & Costello, Allen's show rarely beat Sullivan's in the ratings.

After a few years, Allen's show was cancelled, but he appeared on game shows and continued to create and host new TV shows over the years (where he gave starts to Don Knotts, Steve Lawrence and Edie Gorme, Lenny Bruce, Bob Dylan, Frank Zappa, Albert Brooks and Steve Martin). He once had author Jack Kerouac read his work on the air while Allen played jazz piano, mimicking a Greenwich Village poetry reading. Many of today's comics and TV hosts, including David Letterman, Steve Martin and Robin Williams, credit Allen's TV shows as inspiring them. (TRAIT #12)

In 1977, he created the TV series *Meeting of Minds* for PBS. The show brought together, in a roundtable format, some of the great men and women of history. (TRAIT #4) Allen moderated as host, while actors portrayed such philosophers, scientists and artists as Socrates, Charles Darwin, Attila the Hun, and Galileo. His wife, actress, Jayne Meadows, played historical women such as Emily Dickenson and Marie Antoinette.

---

[2] "Inside a Funny Man Called Steve Allen There's a Private Think Tanks Working Overtime" by Lois Armstrong, People, 3/7/77, v. 7, issue 9, p. 64

TRAIT #4 - I merge my left brain and my right brain; TRAIT #12 - I shape the future

In addition to his TV career, Allen was also a musician and songwriter. His biggest hit, "This Could Be the Start of Something Big," has been recorded by many top artists. He had such a boundless passion for composing songs that he wrote nearly 8,500 songs in his career. (TRAIT #9) The Guinness Book of World Records listed him as the most prolific songwriter of modern times, and many of his songs have been recorded by Judy Garland, Andy Williams, Perry Como and others. (He once won a bet with singer Frankie Laine, when Allen claimed he could write fifty songs a day for a week; Allen managed the feat, writing the songs while sitting in the display window of a Hollywood music store.)

As a musician, he performed in venues as varied as the Roxy on Sunset in Los Angeles to Avery Fisher Hall in New York's Lincoln Center.

Allen also wrote several books over his lifetime, from academic, non-fiction explorations of serious issues, such as the lives of immigrant farmworkers *(The Ground is Our Table)* to a series of light-hearted mystery novels.

But Steve Allen wasn't just a TV host, comedian, author and songwriter. By the mid-70s, he was deeply involved in the academic field of general semantics (a scientific discipline designed to test assumptions, beliefs and language) (TRAIT #2), and he wrote the prefaces to several books published by the Institute of General Semantics.

In his Forward to *Thinking Creatically*, by Kenneth Johnson, Allen explained how he never forgot how he felt at a demonstration of kids who had been taught general semantics. Each of them took a newspaper article or advertisement, read it aloud, and then analyzed it. "The insight, the clarity, the brilliance with which those children

TRAIT #2 - I am insatiably curious; TRAIT #9 - I am passionate separated hot air from factual, reasonable statements was tremendously exciting." He went on to hope that these skills could be taught to the next generation of young Americans. [3]

Allen participated in many an IGS seminar-workshop in Santa Barbara, CA. "To me," he told *People*, "that's like what old Athens must have been in its golden age. You can sit by the ocean in the sunlight and chat with great scholars from around the world."[4] (TRAIT #5)

He included a chapter on general semantics in his 1989 book, *Dumbth*, about the dumbing down of Americans Culture and Americans. 'I have a philosophical concern that the American public is getting dumber," he told the *New York Times* in 1981. ''As we sit here engaged in idle banter, the American public is getting dumber."[5]

Allen got involved with politics at the age of 30, and was involved in many of the political issues of the day, being staunchly anti-bomb, anti-death penalty, and an avid supporter of civil right and women's rights.

Not long before he died, he told the *Los Angeles Times*, "In some ways, I feel more active now than I did many years ago. I feel like I always have. Energetic. Very, very involved." [6]

But he never felt comfortable taking credit for any of his achievements. "Creative gifts are essentially mysterious," he mused to the Archive of American Television. "Not only my own, which I don't understand myself, but if you're talking about the true geniuses, even on

---

[3] "Forward to Thinking Creatically" by Steve Allen, republished in *ETC.: A Review of General Semantics,* Spring 2001, v. 58, Issue 1, p. 15

[4] *People*

[5] "Steve Allen, the Conglomerate" *NY Times*, Feb 16 1981, D.1.

[6] "Steve Allen, TV Innovator, Author, Composer, Dies at 78," by Stephanie Simon, *Los Angeles Times*, Nov 1, 2000, A.1.

---

TRAIT #5 - I delight in sharing what I do

the level of the Leonardos and Shakespeares and Einsteins, nobody has ever been able to explain—and I do mean nobody, not the professional philosophers, not the theologians, not the psychologists—has ever been able to explain why some people are awfully good at certain things. But even those of us who are less gifted, as in my case, while you do have to do your homework, the main thing is the gift. So I've never felt at all comfortable being complimented for anything I can do because it was all easy, and I don't think we really deserve to take deep bows for stuff that we can just laugh off."[7]

---

[7] Archive of American Television

# CONCLUSION

W e began this book by making a distinction between being a genius and being a Renaissance Man. The Renaissance Man can certainly be a genius, but not all geniuses are Renaissance Men. Renaissance Men have intelligence and keen minds, certainly, but instead of putting these at the service of a singular gift, they are driven to expand ever outward in their hunger to explore multiple avenues of expression. We believe we have established in this book that it takes a special personality, a special set of synergistic traits to make a Renaissance Man. And we hope, by codifying these traits, we have enabled you, our reader, to gain a deeper understanding of these remarkable individuals and, perhaps, yourself.

We all have an innate admiration for the multi-faceted man. Think of Sherlock Holmes, the famous detective created by Sir Arthur Conan Doyle, and even how that character has evolved further in the recent Guy Ritchie directed versions. Holmes is intellectually brilliant, yes, but he also possesses physical prowess, is a talented violin player, a man of many disguises, and a profound observer of human nature. His curiosity is voracious, and his perseverance legendary. And he challenges the status quo at every turn. Sherlock is his own man, completely original and true to himself. He is the iconic Renaissance Man laid down in literature, and in film after film adaptation. Why do we keep resurrecting his character? What is the appeal? Well, in our opinion it feeds an archetypical need in us to be many things—to expand beyond labels, to be complex, passionate, driven, innovative, provocative. We'd like to shake up the world with our insights and discoveries. We'd like to make a difference.

In other words, we would all like to be Renaissance Men.

Although most of us will not attain the full state of Renaissance-ness, can we not strive for it? And in the striving, challenge ourselves to be more than we thought we could?

If we look at our modern Renaissance Men, we realize that often it is not in following the crowd but in breaking the mold, in following the imperatives of our own passions, that true innovation arises. Elon Musk making commerical flights into space a reality. Yvon Chouinard demonstrating how a successful business can also be environmentally sound. Dave Stewart merging his left and right brains to spark new ways to look at business, entertainment, and the Internet. Richard Branson bringing together great minds to tackle the world's biggest challenges. John Paul DeJoria showing us that helping others brings the deepest rewards. Frank Nuovo knowing that technology and great design go hand in hand. Steve Jobs expressing his uncanny vision by building diverse, talented teams to manifest that vision. Steve Allen heralding in whole new styles of entertainment. Quincy Jones proving that creativity can expand ever outward. Each of these men refused to be labeled or bound by arbitrary limits. And each of these men can motivate us to dig deeper and push ourselves further. By examining how the twelve traits manifest in our own lives, we can become more of who we are and who we wish to be. The traits, in other words, can be a prism through which we can evaluate, develop and appreciate not only our own Renaissance potential, but that of others, as well.

Furthermore, Renaissance Men can teach us to re-examine some of our most entrenched assumptions. Is, for example, our modern society's near obsession with specialization not always so beneficial? The sciences, academics, even business have become increasingly more narrow where specialties now have subspecialties. This cuts off not only an individual's capacity to flourish in a number of fields, but the free flow of ideas and creativity that happens when different disciplines cross-pollinate.

In education as well, there are lessons to be learned from the Renaissance Men. That, for example, the best thinkers are not always the most academic. That creativity and divergent thinking are as important, perhaps even more important, than doing well on tests. And that, as we spot some of the Renaissance traits in our young people, instead of squelching and discouraging the ones that don't seem to fit the standard education mold, we should praise and encourage them.

We also realize that the traits discussed in this book can and should be used as a launching point for further exploration into the Renaissance mind and how it works. Brain research alone could open up a whole new avenue of study. We can only benefit from learning and understanding more about this fascinating subject.

It is our hope that this book has made you consider some of these issues and more. And that the Renaissance ideal first extolled by Leon Batista Alberti is an ideal that can and will inspire us all.

# ACKNOWLEDGEMENTS

DAVE CARPENTER —

*For believing in me and my many projects.*
*His continued support for the cause of building the 18/8 brand –*
*representing 'Man at His Best'*


ERIC ELFMAN —

*My co-author, co-enthusiast, and effervescent story teller*


LORETTA GRIFFITHS —

*My wife of 30+ years – enabler of this complex and crazy RenMan in*
*the making*
*For saying "yes, go for it" in the very beginning*

FRANK NUOVO —

*Continued enthusiasm and supporter from the beginning of the project*

DAVE STEWART —

*For recognizing the value of the theme, contributing his talents and good name to the cause*

ALLISON BOND —

*Dave's assistant who treated us like a member of the Weapons of Mass Entertainment family*

DALE GRIFFITHS STAMOS —

*For bringing her superb editing and writing skills to the project and putting a beautiful bow around the package to bring it home*

ALEXA ESPINOZA —

*A Renaissance woman in training – my bright, talented, and delightful teaching, research, design assistant*

RON LOVE —

*My longtime business partner, and co-founder of 18/8 – for trusting me to take the ball and run with it*

BRIGITTE THEWES LOVE —

*The person who delivers on the 18/8 promise…helping men to look better, feel better, so they can perform better*

JOHN BUCKINGHAM —

*Longtime professor at Pepperdine University Graziadio School of Business, for being my mentor and supporter at the University*


*And, of course, to all the RenMen of the past, present, and future, God knows we need so many more of you*

# ABOUT THE AUTHORS

**W. Scott Griffiths**

Scott Griffiths has been building companies and directing successful brands for twenty years, including for Paul Mitchell ("Mitch for Men"), House of Blues, Crystal Cruises, Nokia and Vertu, just to name a few. He has led or was on the leadership team of twenty start-ups and early stage companies. He is the CEO and Founder of 18/8 Fine Men's Salons (www.EighteenEight.com), and is also a professor at Pepperdine University Graziadio School of Business and Management.

He describes his years growing up as idyllic. When he was 11 – 13 years old, while his father "Griff Griffiths" was working on his PhD in Middle Eastern Studies- with a specialty on the Ottoman Empire- Scott, along with his twin sister, Dale, lived throughout Europe, including a year in Istanbul. In each country, they would study the languages and learn about the culture. In Istanbul, while attending Robert College Community School, the elementary-secondary school which was an off shoot of the local prestigious American College, he studied Turkish, a requirement of which was to learn and read the Koran. Every weekend, by himself, Scott would take a taxi cab into the old city, and wander the bazaars. Over time he got to know every shop keeper, and with many of them he would share desserts (baklava) and Turkish tea. Later, when his father created Semester at Sea, a university on a ship that spends each semester visiting twelve countries, Scott went on one of the voyages and had a chance to travel throughout Africa and Asia. His consulting businesses have also brought Scott more international exposure and an opportunity to work with some of the best business leaders around the world.

During his early years he was immersed in a variety of sports (surfing, tennis, volleyball, waterpolo, swimming, and skiing). He was also an entrepreneur from a young age, starting with taking care of people's gardens; then as he became an artist/painter, selling his paintings at street fares. Most of his teachers, even the principal of his high school, bought his paintings.

Scott receive his B.A. from Chapman University and then graduated as a scholarship student from Art Center College of Design, where he later served as President of the Alumni Board. While attending Art Center, he worked with his father in the marketing department at Semester at Sea. He went on to pursue his MBA from the UCLA Anderson School. He is a past member of the Harvard Business School Association of Orange County, where he helped direct the marketing of the annual Entrepreneurs Conference for 12 years. He has served as marketing advisor to the UCLA Anderson Economic Forecast, has taught at Chapman University Business School, and currently teaches at Pepperdine Graziadio School of Business and Management, in the area of International Marketing and Marketing Management. He is a member of the University of California Irvine Chief Executive Roundtable, and sits on the Board of Directors for the Surfing Heritage & Cultural Center (www.surfingheritage.org). Scott is the author of five books published by Random House, Doubleday, and Little Brown. Two of his books – "Air Powered," and "America's Best Beers" were best sellers.

# Eric Elfman

Eric Elfman is the award-winning author of twelve books, including *Tesla's Attic*, the first in a three-book series of middle grade novels he co-wrote, to be published by Disney-Hyperion Books starting in 2014. His other books include three bestselling, offbeat almanacs for Random House (one of them named an *ALA Recommended Book for Reluctant Readers*), three novelizations for HarperCollins, and two books of short stories for Lowell House.

Several of Eric's books have been optioned for development by TV and film production companies, including Merv Griffin Enterprises, Triage Entertainment, and Al Burton Productions (producers of *Win Ben Stein's Money*).

Also a screenwriter, Eric has written screenplays for Interscope Pictures (*You Should See the Conklins' Living Room*), Walden Media (*As You Like It (Revisited)*), and Universal Studios (*Curious George: The Sequel*). Eric and his writing partner sold an original pitch, *Class Act,* to Revolution Studios. Their screenplay was later set up at Dreamworks with Halle Berry attached to star.

For television, Eric provided the English-language dialogue for several Japanese *animé* series. He also wrote the host banter for THE STAR KIDS CHALLENGE, a competition show featuring the young leads of television's hit sit-coms, which was taped at Universal Studios Hollywood in front of a live audience.

For the past eight years, Eric has coached over 100 authors in workshops and privately, many of whom have subsequently had their books published (including four in 2012). Since 2005, he has been on the faculty of the Big Sur Writers Workshop, sponsored by the Henry Miller Library and directed by Andrea Brown.

Eric led the development of an innovative fifth grade social studies curriculum for the Galef Institute, incorporating modern theories of learning and emphasizing movement, dance, music, art, literature, and creative thinking. He also wrote study guides for P.L.A.Y. (Performing for Los Angeles Youth) for the Center Theatre Group at the Los Angeles Music Center. Each study guide, aimed at teachers of Los Angeles high school and middle school students, introduced the concepts of theatre and the themes of the play performed.

Eric has also contributed articles to *Global Trade Magazine*, *Dwell*, *Mental Floss*, and other magazines, and has conducted interviews with Hollywood's top screenwriters for *Creative Screenwriting Magazine*.

CPSIA information can be obtained at www.ICGtesting.com
Printed in the USA
BVOW08*0747300516

450044BV00002B/3/P